FUNN STUFF

by KARL ROHNKE

KENDALL/HUNT PUBLISHING COMPANY
4050 Westmark Drive   Dubuque, Iowa 52002

All photos by K.E. Rohnke
Illustrations by Johneen Kissler

Copyright © 1996 by Karl E. Rohnke

ISBN 0-7872-1633-X

Printed in the United States of America
10   9   8   7   6   5   4   3

CONTENTS

Trust, 39

Variations, 53

Ropes Course Construction and Implementation, 63

SYMBOLS

The following symbols appropriately found near the title of each activity, should be used as a guideline for the way the activity is *usually* done.

Activity Level

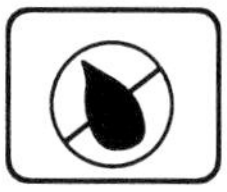

No sweat

Some sweat

Top sweat

Activity Area

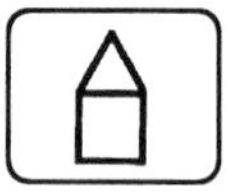

Indoor

Outdoor

Indoor/Outdoor

Props

P   Props needed

P/2   Some props needed

No props needed

FUNN STUFF INTRODUCTION

Some of you used to subscribe to an adventure curriculum quarterly that I wrote called *Bag of Tricks*. If that's true, welcome to the new BOT's format called **Funn Stuff**. A majority of my other books had the word BAG in the title somewhere and things were getting confusing — *Bottomless Bag, Bottomless Baggie, Bottomless Bag Again, Bag of Tricks....* I was even thinking of *Baggettes* for the next book, but enough is enough.

The word **FUNN** is simply a whimsical acronym and an obvious play on words: **F**unctional **U**nderstanding's **N**ot **N**ecessary. It's obvious that understanding *is* necessary if you're trying to accomplish something, but the light hearted suggestion of "not understanding" indicates that it's OK to occasionally have fun for no other reason than experiencing laughter and enjoyable time together.

If you are a new reader and curious, here's an abridged historical sketch of where this all started, otherwise turn the page and lets get into the games.

Cowstails and Cobras was published in 1977. During the two following years I continued collecting and writing about ideas in the field of adventure education. With overflowing files, I launched *Bag of Tricks* in December of 1979 as a vehicle for sharing those ideas.

I started out in "79" with less than 100 subscribers, paying a yearly four-issue subscription rate of 5 dollars. BOT's was never a big money maker, but it paid for itself and allowed me to work on something that was creatively satisfying, in addition, people said they enjoyed reading the text.

Around 1983 I decided to collect all the back issues of BOT's and develop the copy into book form, which eventually became Project Adventure's best seller, *Silver Bullets*. The ideas kept

coming, I kept writing, and a book appeared every couple years since then.

But after 64 non-stop issues I'd had enough hands-on journalism — typing labels, licking stamps and envelope stuffing. I checked in with Kendall/Hunt Publishing Co. to see if they would like to spiff up BOT's (photographs, illustrations, book format) and print a few. They said yes, so here we are at the beginning of a new series of adventure curriculum books that will be available on a biyearly basis, as long as the ideas, profitability (Kendall/Hunt doesn't do this just for fun) and my interest continue.

Welcome to FUNN STUFF #1. You can say you were there! Me too!

Karl E. Rohnke; June, 1995

DISCLAIMER

Disclaimers are not what I would call interesting reading, but you better read it because...

❏ Adventure curricula or activities should not be undertaken without the supervision of leaders who have successfully completed qualified professional instruction in the use of the skills necessary to implement adventure curricula or activities.

❏ Instruction and suggestions in this book for the construction and implementation of ropes course elements are subject to varying interpretations and the construction process is an inexact science.

❏ Before any attempt is made to use any ropes course elements whose construction has incorporated any of the materials contained in this book, a qualified professional should determine that safe techniques have been employed in their construction thereafter. Inspections by a qualified professional no less frequently than annually should be made to protect users against accident or injury that

**Look out
more Funn comin' at ya!**

Adventure Games

Why Adventure Games? Mostly because I needed a title for this section and it *is* what the staff at Project Adventure calls this stuff.

It's has been a bit confusing over the years differentiating between Adventure Games and New Games. The *New Game Foundation* began playing games in 1974 I believe (give or take a year). Whoever decided to call these zany, imaginative activities NEW GAMES was a marketing genius; the term really caught on and is still used as a catch phrase for any activity that isn't nailed down by a traditional name, e.g. baseball, hockey, etc.

Project Adventure began operation in 1971 and as part of the developing adventure curriculum, the staff was making up and using new games before there was a *New Games*. It doesn't matter what you call these curriculum gems, they "work", and working in this context means that the people involved are cooperating, communicating and trusting one another while playing rather than competing to win.

The *New Games* trainers used to say, "Play Hard. Play Fair. Nobody Hurt."; makes sense to me. It's my personal feeling that there's nothing wrong with a bit of competition as long as the win/lose thing isn't overemphasized. Competition against self or a nebulous goal adds some zing and spice to the activity. If there has to be a winner (everybody feels good) and loser (everybody feels bad) then it's time to let the varsity folks duke it out. Competitive sports are OK for people who want to compete at that level (and are capable), but what about some activities for folks who just want to play. Here's a few *new* games for the players.

Ah-So-Ko

Ah-So-Ko involvement is a well played example of the FUNN concept (Functional Understanding's Not Necessary). Get into it, enjoy the time, and don't worry about why you're laughing.

I have been using this game for years, but for some reason never wrote it up, so I did and here 'tis.

This game was adapted from an activity called *Zen Clap* in **The New**

1

Games Book. I'm also sure I remember a game very similar to this one, played in college, which involved a considerable amount of beer consumption...

The Presentation or Setting the Group Up —

Arrange your group of 10 to 25 in a sitting circle on the ground, grass, or floor. Explain in a serious manner (using a tone they all respect and go along with, but strongly suspect you're putting them on), that everyone is about to take part in a symbolic martial arts encounter, emphasizing that the movements and sounds they are about to learn are steeped in ancient tradition. Fighting a smile, indicate that the karate movements are real but symbolic, so that no one gets hurt.

Ask everyone to make a striking implement of their open hand (essentially holding either hand as if you were about to render a salute; palm down) and to bring that hand swiftly toward their own throat, stopping well short of corporal contact and gutturally exclaiming **"AAH!"** Try that movement and associated sound with the group, histrionically displaying what you would like them to mime and vocalize.

That's movement and sound #1. Number two involves the same hand, but this time the knife strike is aimed directly between the eyes. Inexplicably you miss and the open palmed hand flies directly over your head accompanied by the chagrined and simultaneous lament of **"SSO!"** Repeat that movement and sound a couple times with the group. Emphasize fast abrupt movements and deep throated husky exclamations.

Remember you are setting up your players for some off-the-wall fun, and to do this takes some time and personal energy to get them in the mood. You need to explicitly grant permission to play by demonstrating how to be acceptably zany.

The last gesture and sound is based on the obvious miss of the over-the-head knife strike movement. In a paroxysm of embarrassment the humbled player tries to transfer the shame to another player by pointing at someone (anyone—make direct eye contact) with their open hand, exclaiming condemningly, **"KO!"**

Let's return briefly to the first movement and sound to review how these three sounds and movements blend together in the game format. When the game initiator says **AH!**, bringing the knife-strike hand toward their own throat, notice that the extended fingers are pointed to the player either to their right or left in the seated circle configuration. The pointed-at-player must respond immediately by flailing their right or left hand above their head (using the proper hand strike/salute positioning) and exclaiming **SO!** Again, the player is pointing either to the right or left. The third player in this *ménage* must use their open palmed hand to point to anyone in the circle and say **KO!** Whoever receives this definitive pointing movement must either (1) Begin the sequence again with dispatch by saying **AH!** and striking toward their throat, or, (2) Crossing his/her hands directly in front of their face (palms out) and

shouting **NO!** If the NO! command is delivered, the person who just pointed saying KO! must begin the AH! sequence immediately.

Allow the group to practice a bit before beginning the game, then explain this following final fillip of facetious facts. *Mistakes of any kind are not allowed in this ancient martial arts game.* The charter group of mauve belt practitioners would be aghast otherwise. If a mistake is recognized by the group, each player must condemningly thrust their fist forward onto their thigh, with thumb erect. In unison, so that there is no doubt in the offending player's mind, each player shouts at the top of their lungs, **"Y'ER OUTTA THE GAME!!!"**, simultaneously jerking their fist and finger up and over their shoulder.

As that vilified person removes themselves from the honored circle, their conspicuous and embarrassing gap is immediately filled and closed by the remaining players. The person to the removed player's left then has five

seconds to initiate a new AH! movement or they are also **OUTTA THE GAME!** In keeping with Project Adventure's commitment to maintain a playful profile, the rudely ejected players take on a new role as DH's; i.e., Designated Harassers. These rudely discarded players circle the circle, harassing whom they please, trying to get even by causing someone to make a mistake. Their bothersome presence does not include physical contact of any kind, nor can they block the vision of a player, otherwise anything (be decent) goes.

The last two remaining players represent an endangered species, and it is their responsibility to wander off into the sunset together to repopulate the earth. The final two players should be chosen wisely.

Was that *funn*, or what?

Remember, the level of fun and enjoyment associated with this old "drinking game" depends largely upon your animated presentation of the rules and your continued active and vocal participation during the game itself.

Blindman's Cannonball Bluff a.k.a. The Tank

Objective: To have lots of loud uninhibited fun throwing things at people, combined with an excellent chance of not hitting anyone — and to be the last pair remaining.

When the game starts you better follow these rules — or you're going to have to make up some of your own.

❑ Players operate as pairs; i.e., multiple teams of dyads. Decide twixt you and your dyadinous partner who's going to wear the available blindfold. You can also ask the players to "go bare" (no blindfold) then, "Cross their hearts and hope to die!" if they take a peek, but you know they will, so to keep the mortality rate under control say it's OK; 'cause it is — Really!

❑ Give each pair two fleece balls. **DO NOT USE TENNIS BALLS!**

❑ After the GO signal, the blindfolded player tries to hit (the ball must be thrown) either member of another pair. Bounces off the floor don't count. If either of the dyad are hit, that pair must switch roles or be eliminated from play — your compassionate choice.

❑ The sighted player may not touch the balls or their partner. It is his/her role to only offer verbal directions.

Play continues until lunch or one pair remains. I suppose one of the pair should say, "Yeah, we won!" Then begin play again smartly by having the partnersexchange roles. That's a typo; take a closer look ...*partners exchange roles*. Oh sure, *now* it's OK...

Why did we play this game? Come on, how long have you known me? Because it's *funn*, and good things happen when people are having fun.

Are the partner players cooperating? Is communication being stressed? Is trust a factor when blindfolded? Yes, Yes, YES! Why did we play this game? Geez!...

Cacophony

Arrange your group into a square (rectangle's OK) holding hands, including yourself as part of the square. If the group is too young to handle holding hands, don't hold hands.

You start the action by making a distinctive sound (whistle, clucking, whoop, Braaaaap) and continue that sound. Shortly thereafter (about 1.75 seconds) squeeze the hand of the person

to your left, (since we are largely a counterclockwise society, squeeze clockwise just to be ornery). When the person feels the squeeze they begin producing their unique sound, then keeping to the not-so-exact 1.75 second pause, the next squeeze and sound is passed along.

Soon the entire group will be producing a continuous cacophonic chorus unlike anything that you or they have ever heard. When the noise has saturated each person's cochlea, turn down the volume by initiating the squeeze for another round, at the same time cutting off your auditory contribution. As each person gets the squeeze, they also reduce their personal decibels to zero. If this is still confusing think of it as a sound wave; i.e., like the WAVE that flows through a football stadium crowd.

It's kind of like hitting your head against the sound barrier; when you quit it sounds pretty good.

WHY? Because it's zany, requires cooperation, alerts the students that anything's possible, and what's next?

Face Value

Retrieved from the land of OZ on a recent trip *down under* by Lee Gillis, and named over a *Honey Brown Ale*. **Face Value** follows the verbal lead of "passing a secret" in a much more histrionic and entertaining manner.

Line up a group in such a way that two single files of participants lead away from your position as the apex of an obtuse **V**, with everyone in the two lines also facing away from you. Indicate that the two people closest to you in the **V** are to turn around on a signal (shoulder tap) and closely observe how you are representing yourself — facial features, body position, gestures, etc. — then turn back to their initial positions and signal to the person in front of them to about-face so the new pair (second pair) can do their own observation of how the first pair have reproduced your initial presentation.

The two lines are essentially and sequentially passing along, morphologically and auditorially, whatever you initially instigate. Whatever you decide to initiate, make sure it's super simple.

When the last pair have had a chance to "take a look", they should turn toward the group and demonstrate what they received as a representation of what you initiated, then display to all what you showed to the initial pair. Needless to say the results are often vastly different and invariably humorous.

As a variation, and to accommodate more people, set up four lines as a **W**. The final four players eventually demonstrate to one another (and the entire group) what has been passed along to them, and is now so vastly different.

Faux Flicker Ball

This fast moving gymnasium game has been around for quite awhile, but Carol Call (PA Trainer from Georgia) tweaked the rules a bit, adding to the fun.

Things you need:

- ❑ a basketball court or the like
- ❑ two hula hoops (large hoops make scoring easier)
- ❑ one 8″ dense foam ball
- ❑ two teams — not chosen by the two best athletes or two best friends

Rules and such:

❑ The hula hoops are put over the basket hoops so that they hang down partially below the backboards. The vertical hoops represent the goal areas.
❑ The game starts with a throw-off, which is the equivalent of a kick-off in football.
❑ The object is for the opposing team to score a goal by throwing the ball through the opponent's hula hoop. After a goal has been scored, play is begun again with a throw-off.
❑ A player may pass, slap, or kick the ball in any direction and may also run sideways or backward, but may not run forward while holding the ball.

❑ A player has only five seconds ± to pass the ball, or the ball goes over to the other side.
❑ You may defend a player as you would in basketball, but you may not strike the ball out of another player's grasp.
❑ If you are in a gym that has four baskets, put up four hula hoops, add another foam ball to the action, and go with four teams. Designate who should score where or scoring will be indiscriminate. Hey, wait... that sounds like a good idea.
❑ Carol suggests using a GUAC ball to slow down the better athletes. If you don't know what a Guac ball is, never mind.
❑ You may either "play 'til you puke", or until tea is served.

Fill Me In

A name *reminder* game; i.e., don't play this game until the participants have, at an earlier time, tossed each other's names around.

Line up in a circle again. (Why are we so circle oriented in the games we play and activities we pursue? 'Cause it works better than a square, and lots better than a rhombus.) The diameter of the circle should be such that it would take about ten steps to cross; say, thirty feet.

You begin the action by stepping into the circle, simultaneously announcing someone's name that is directly opposite your position, then walk toward the person. That verbally named person must immediately duplicate your action by identifying another person in the circle, saying their name, and begin walking toward that person's position. So each named person ends up heading toward another player's position.

Establish eye contact with the person who's name you call in order to make sure that the player recognizes their immediate responsibility to move out and name another person on the way. This is not the time to say, Uhhh... well... uhhh...

After the action has established itself, ask the two moving people to briefly shake hands and exchange first names at the crossing.

If the group knows each other well, initiate the game with two people starting off. If it's still too easy, suggest walking faster or start a third person. Emphasize the need for compassionate movement and occasional *bumpers up*.

End the game with lots of people calling out names combined with a chaotic combination of crossings.

Flashback

Remember *Backstabber* (**Bottomless Bag Again ?!**; pg. 90)? If you liked Backstabber but were hard put to find the clothespin props, try *Flashback*. Chris Cavert passed this game variation along, and it seems like a good one.

❑ Create some real or existential boundaries for the players who need them.
❑ Arrange your players more or less inside the boundaries.
❑ Hand out one fleece ball per participant and say GO!

If it's obvious that a bit more game guidance is needed, explain that a player remains in the game as long as they do not get hit on the back with a fleece ball. Experiencing a dorsal hit, the struck player is OUT OF THE GAME, or the back hit can be counted as a point toward a team total — your competitive choice.

I just thought of a variation that might result in more action and spontaneous team work — Half the group starts as *back-whackers* and the other half are *front-loaders*. The back-whackers try to hit the front-loaders in the back with a ball causing them to immediately change affiliation. The front-loaders try to hit the back-whackers on the front of the torso, with an identical change of loyalty. In this way no one is eliminated, and at the end of say five very aerobic minutes, call a halt and find out which team has the most viable members. The game may end sooner if one team has more rocket-armed participants, but don't underestimate the power of sneaky.

A player may try to knock down or block the throw of an opponent only if the throw is against a team member. No one may attempt to block a throw made at themselves; in that case only dodging and evasive action is allowed. Head shots don't count.

Sounds like a fun game. Yeah Chris! Yeah Karl! You're welcome... you're welcome.

Global Ball

In the July, 94 issue of Camping Connections from The Camping Association of Victoria (Australia), comes *Global Ball*. This game was apparently offered by Marcel Goudriaan of Holland who was, at the time, serving an internship at *Project Adventure Australia*.

Many years ago in *Bag of Tricks*, I reported on a game, like Global Ball, that required players on two teams to throw tennis balls at an Earth Ball (Cage Ball) with the intention of knocking the large ball over a goal line. I don't think the game caught on because of the potential for injury caused by hard thrown tennis balls. But Global Ball circumvents that problem by using fleece balls instead of tennis balls and a large beach ball instead of a cage ball. Marcel does mention using tennis balls as an alternative, but I'd recommend against their use.

A couple rules and recommendations:

❑ No obstruction of balls (large or small) allowed.

❑ This is a no physical contact game; i.e., no hip checking, blocking or hands-on of any kind.

❑ Start from behind the respective goal lines, with the beach ball placed at midfield for the start.

❑ Use an agreed upon minimum distance that the thrower must be away from the Beach Ball before throwing. This distance requirement can be loosely enforced, but it keeps players from getting so close to the ball that they might "inadvertently" bump the ball toward their goal.

❑ If someone does move the Beach Ball with any part of their body, the other team gets three unblocked throws by three different players. These three penalty throws must be completed within 10 seconds of the penalty announcement or the three throws are forfeit.

❑ Try starting off with two fleece balls per person and require that a player

can have no more than two balls in their possession during the action.

❑ There is no out-of-bounds area, so players may run to pick up any thrown fleece ball no matter where it ends up.

❑ There is also no stopping of play, because if a goal is scored, the scored upon team is allowed to immediately pick up the ball, run to the mid-stripe and smack the ball once with an open hand toward their goal line. This is a "free kick" and cannot be blocked by the other team.

I changed the rules somewhat from the original, but then, so should you.

Hoop Me Rhonda!

Eric Johnson (Vergennes, VT) sent me the basic rules for this simple but effective hula hoop activity, and graciously offered credit to Bill Clark and Eric Vantassel as the originators. I've tried this activity with a couple groups; it's a winner.

In teams of three, designate one person as the "Hole", another person as the "Thrower" and the third person as "Comptroller". The object for that troika is to move a hula hoop from one point to another (say, 30 yards) AFAP (As Fast As Possible), while other groups of three are trying to do the same with their own hoop and strategies.

Rules: (without which chaos reigns — not a bad way to be occasionally)

❑ The *Hole* person and *Thrower* are either blindfolded (see photo) or have their eyes clamped tight with CBC (Challenge By Choice) stickum.

❑ The *Comptroller* remains sighted, but is not allowed to touch the hoop, *ever*.

❑ The hoop must be *thrown* from *Thrower* to *Hole*, not simply passed.

The throwing distance is up to the players.

❑ A catch is designated as successful if the hoop does not touch the ground after leaving the *Thrower's* hands. The *Hole* person can arrange their body in whatever configuration or position that seems to increase their chance of keeping the hoop off the ground.

❑ A missed throw must be returned to the *Thrower* for another try. The

Comptroller can assist this process, but only verbally.

❑ All three players are allowed to communicate freely.

Afterward:

❑ Talk about how techniques differed, notwithstanding what place they arrived at the destination. Did the competition aspect detract from the exercise?

❑ What worked best; consistently trying a long throw, sticking with a predictable short toss, or perhaps a combination of the two? Ask if any group started with one method and changed their technique as the result of what they were experiencing en route.

❑ How did the communication differ from group to group?

❑ Would the groups like to try again? Would they like to try and figure out a way that all the teams could work together to establish a large group "World Record"?

Look Up/Look Down

Refer to *Caught Ya Peekin'* (**The Bottomless Bag Again ?!**; pg. 125) for a variation of this quickie but very enjoyable game.

Standing in a shoulder-to-shoulder circle, the group is instructed to all "Look down". When the command "Look Up" is given, all must do so simultaneously, looking directly at the eyes of any other player. If any pair catch themselves looking at one another, they are both out of the game. If a player ends up looking at a player who's looking at someone else, both players are still in the game.

The object is to remain in the game as long as possible, but as luck would have it (there's very little skill associated with this game) eye contact eventually happens, except for the last person remaining in the game — the WINNER!

Sometimes there is no winner, with two finalists remaining. Without missing a beat, ask the final pair to, "Look down", then "Look up." As they incredulously look at one another or at you, declare the game a draw.

This game does not work well with a group that is still working through the apparent paradox of being able to enjoy a game without having to WIN. Help them with this transition. Isn't that your *fun*ction?

Jumpin', Shuckin', Twirlin' — Medley Relay

So simple, spontaneous, usable, physical...

Divide your group into teams of 5-7, and start them at one end of a grassy football pitch. Avoid artificial turf, basketball courts, hard packed dirt areas, or parking lots.

Indicate the various ways that are allowed to make forward progress. Let the group decide who's going to choose which technique. Each team establishes their own PB (Personal Best) then tries to better their last best effort; intense competition at its best.

Here's a few sanctioned forward progress movements toward establishing the team's PB. Choose movements that seems appropriate for your group, or better yet, make some up that everyone agrees to try.

All efforts are closely measured, then the totals are added together. Use a stretched section of 1/4" bungee cord staked out on the turf as a starting line.

If you are shuckin'-n-jumpin' in a gym, use a section of colored tape for the start. Remember to arrange cushioned pads for a landing area.

- ❑ one footed jump; right or left foot — if this is the first movement, a running start is allowed.
- ❑ one footed jump, left or right — no running start.
- ❑ two footed jump forward or backward.
- ❑ forward dive and roll — measure where the person first makes contact with the turf. Don't allow this attempt unless the group has had some practice with the forward shoulder roll.
- ❑ cartwheel
- ❑ 10 seconds of forward progress on your glutes — gluteus maximus contact with the floor only.
- ❑ no-step vault with a pole — only if this relay is being attempted on turf.

❏ holding your toes with both hands and not releasing during the forward jump.

❏ standing-start jump with a minimum 360° turn in the air. Jumper must remain standing after the attempt. This contest is most fun at the beach.

Plunging The Depths of Psyche Center

If you're anticipating a sophisticated one-on-one encounter-type activity as related to the caption above, stop anticipating. This face-to-face encounter is much more earthy, definitely of the toilet variety.

The Set Up

Get yourself a one inch by 18" dowel and affix two new (straight from the store) toilet plungers to each end.

Make a small slit (use a sharp, pointed, lock-back knife) in a used tennis ball. Put a bulky-type knot in the end of a 16" section of small diameter cord. A bulky-type knot is properly fashioned by tying twice (maybe three times) whatever knot comes to mind. Open the slit in the ball like you would open a change purse and shove that speciality knot into the slit.

Tie the other end of the string/cord to the center of the dowel. This is probably best tied with a strangle or constrictor knot. If you can't remember how to manipulate those specific knots, tie it on with multiple repeats of whatever knot you do remember.

The Procedure

Ask a consenting couple (plunger partners) to rest their foreheads on the cup portion of the plunger so that they are looking directly at one another. Is this going to involve cooperation and communication? Correct-a-mundo! You didn't think I'd have you blatantly competing against someone using a toilet plunger, ...did you?

With the plungers in place and the ball dangling down, ask the two primed participants to wind the cord around the dowel so that the ball eventually ends up in permanent contact with the dowel. *Hands and arms cannot be used*; only body manipulation and gyrations are allowed. GO! If you need any more rules, make up a few.

Ring on a Rope

Get a section of any kind of small diameter rope (even sash cord will do) and cut a length that measures three times the number of participants in your group + 5 (3 X 15 + 5 = 50 feet). Tie the ends of the rope together using whatever neat-o-knot you remember; nobody's safety depends upon this knot, so do your worst. Distribute the members of your group so that they are inside the rope, standing in a circle, backs to the rope. There should be no more than 12" between people. The volunteer IT person stands in the center of the circle.

The object is to pass the rubber ring... (Nuts, I forgot to tell you to put a rubber deck tennis ring onto the rope before tying the knot. Sorry. Do that now.) ...around the perimeter of the circle without the circle-center person being able to tell where the ring is located. If he/she correctly identifies where the ring is or sees it being moved, the IT person takes the place of the unfortunate player who was caught rubber handed.

This game can be really tedious if the group isn't into working together to hide the movement of the ring. This is not a good *first* game.

Continue playing until you don't want to.

The Snail

I have been a rotating part of Larry Rorick's *Snail* at least twice, and for some reason I keep forgetting to record it. But I obviously remembered, 'cause here we are.

Ask your entire group to join hands (groups of 30-60 people are better than 15) with you at the end or beginning of the line. Begin walking slowly, encouraging others to follow your lead.

Walk in a large circle so that the end of the line eventually ends up near you, (say, *juxtaposed* when you're trying to impress the group) then peel inwards a bit so that you are gradually spiraling toward the center of a diminishing circle. Participants will enjoy the spectacle of bodies zipping past one another and the older participants may even wax nostalgic about grabbing a merry-go-round brass ring!

The spiral will eventually reach a spin-around central point for the lead person — you. Continue rotating until the entire group has formed a tight spiral around one another with you nicely tucked in the center. On a cold day this is a very nice place to be. While slowly rotating, duck down and duck walk under the arms and bodies of the still slowly rotating or vibrating group. Don't forget to take your in-hand partners with you.

Unravel the spiral until you can guide the group back into a circle. Finish with a positive flourish like *Group High Fives*, *The Nice Going Award* or *The Perfect Circle*.

Share smiles, shake some hands, wave goodbye, then go home. Stop facilitating. Give your family a break; it's just a job, you know.

Stars at Night

Get over to Wal-Mart, or any large department-type store, and head for the toy department to find some of those glow-in-the-dark stars that you had over your bed when you were a kid. Not only is it fun and sweetly nostalgic to once again pepper your ceiling with stars, planets and such but there's a pure-dark tag game involving these stars that's bound to cause a few smiles and squirts of epinephrine. Caveat — If you sleep with some one, better talk about reproducing the milky way on your ceiling before you cause some marital/celestial fireworks that makes glow-in-the-dark pale in comparison.

The stars come with a Silly Putty-like stickum that is not permanent, but sticks well enough to keep the celestial symbols on the ceiling for awhile, but more corporally significant, sticks them to your bod. If you sweat a lot better get some clear tape. Stick a big star (they come in various sizes) to your forehead. Occupy a "cleared" dark room with some other like-minded star-stuck folks and play tag, or Zombie, or Prui, or Clam Free.

Clear the darkened room of items that might cause harm to laughing star fighters, particularly those hard items that cause tripping, poking and holes to appear in your body.

No fair covering up your star, but turning your head frequently is allowed. For increased star movement and potential deception, stick a star to the back of each hand. Again, no fair covering up the stars, but flipping your hands over is certainly OK.

Games in the dark represent a significant trust commitment for many players. Let the players choose individually who wants to play, and stay near the light switch in case instant illumination is needed, or to shield it from sneaky players.

Count Coup Swat Tag

CC Swat Tag provides a fine example of how "game change" works. If a game isn't working, change it. If a game *is* working but you want to test it's potential for fun, change it. The original game of *Swat Tag* can be found in **The New Games Book** by Andrew Fluggelman.

Ask your group to surround you as a circle. The players should be at least 20 feet away from you at circle center and have a minimum of 2' between each other.

Designating yourself as IT, you must try to get out of your center position by using the ethafoam bat to swat someone below the waist. That person then follows you (chases you) toward the center of the circle where an Aerobie or a Woosh ring has been placed on the ground. You must put your bat on top of the ring and attempt to get back into the place vacated by the hit player before he/she (now armed with your sword) can hit you. If you make it unscathed into the arc, that person is then IT, and must begin the sequence again by hitting someone else, (no hit-backs allowed).

If you neglected to place your bat carefully on the ring so that it slid or rolled off, the hit person is not required to pick it up, and can casually saunter back to their place in the arc, casting disdainful looks in your direction. You must then contritely pick up the sword and try someone else.

If the person does smite you before you get into the arc, they must then put the sword on the ring and make all haste back to their former place in the arc. Can this action/reaction continue back and forth? Indeed, and often does until one or both players begin to experience oxygen debt.

Explain that if someone gets "caught" in the center and can't get themselves out, all that person has to do is walk up to any other player in the circle, hold out the foam bat, look 'em in the eye and say HELP! That chosen person is then obliged to either help or not help, and the game continues.

Game Change #1 - Ask everyone to hold hands in the circle. (For this aspect of the game to work you will need at least 15 people to play, otherwise the circle is too small.) When you hit someone (play is identical as above) and they vacate their place in the arc, anyone is allowed to run over and fill their place, and then someone can fill that place, etc, etc. Thus, the open place is constantly changing. The reason for holding hands is so that the open place remains apparent.

If you have a bunch of fleece balls or an abundance of any small objects, ask each player to get one and put it on the ground immediately behind where they are standing in the game circle. These objects mark the player's positions and obviate the need for holding hands.

Game Change #2 - Indicate that if the players would like to display their bravery "under fire," so to speak, they can attempt, as the game swirls about them, to enter the inner circle and, dropping to one knee, attempt to touch their forehead to a ring concurrently shouting **COUNT COUP!** If this is accomplished without sustaining an ethafoam bat whack (check out the gluteal target availability of the bent over *Count Coup* positioning), the ultimate game accolades are heaped upon this person by their playmates. If hit, that person reverts to the hit-IT situation as above and the game continues.

By this time, with all the rule variations and people running about willy nilly, a certain level of chaos is usually achieved. With a minimum 8.5 level of play extant, the game becomes a happening, rather an end in itself, and either eventually ends via exhaustion or perpetuates as a Zen continuum of existential play.

The level of play in the basic game can be speeded up by placing a second and sometimes a third bat into play. Make sure you add an additional ring within the circle for each additional bat; two bats, two rings. Bats can be put down on any ring. Why? Why not. It's your game now, do what you want.

It seems obvious, but remember that with more bats and rings in play there will be more people moving rapidly within the circle, often with their heads down. Keep mentioning to the players to fend off one another and care enough for each other to prevent the most common cause of adventure program injuries — running into or tripping over another player.

UDT - Ultimate Deck Tennis

This very active running/passing game is a combination of a variation, of a variation — finest kind.

Object of Play — one rubber deck tennis ring

Area Needed - Basketball court, half a football pitch, or whatever you've got.

Get people used to catching the rubber ring, like in the game *Italian Golf* (**Bottomless Bag Again ?!**, pg. 86), as this over-the-wrist reception is the only way that a team can score. Bring out lots of rings and let the players toss them around for about five minutes. Suggest trying short and long throws, as both

distances will be used during the game. I'm not sure why, but most people love throwing and catching these rings. You will probably have to ask them to quit so you can get the game started.

Split your group into two teams; i.e., in half. Use one of the *Category* (**Bottomless Bag Again!?**, Pg. 143) categories to do this. If the groups don't come out even, substitute other categories until they do. There's no hurry to play this particular game so let the folks have fun dividing up the group, and at the same time finding out some things about themselves and one another. Actually that's an important point; slow down, let the game happen — play!

Hand out head bands or use some other visual technique to differentiate between the two teams. The head bands I use are white panty-hose seconds of which I have hundreds. If you are interested in where to get free panty-hose seconds and other interesting things to do with them, without being branded a pervert, see below.*

Rules for the time being

❑ To score a point a team must throw the rubber ring over either of the end-of-the-field goal lines and have it "speared" by a teammate in the approved, hand-extended, *Italian Golf* gesture. (See photo above)
❑ To qualify for a scoring throw attempt, a team must complete ten consecutive throw-and-catches

* If you would like a LARGE box of panty-hose discards from L'Eggs, do this. Write a letter on your non-profit letter head requesting one box of pantyhose discards. If you feel foolish doing this, reflect on the fact that these folks receive letters like this all the time. They will not think badly of you, honest. The Sara Lee people will respond to your letter telling you want to do from there.

Write to: Sara Lee Hosiery
            L'Eggs Products
            1901 North Irby St.
            Florence SC 29501

without a miss (ring hitting the ground). If, during this 1-10 sequence, the ring is dropped or knocked down, it immediately goes over to the other team.

❑ During this throwing/catching sequence the ring must be thrown; no hand-to-hand passes are allowed.

❑ Players are not allowed to throw the ring back and forth between just two players. The ring must be thrown to a third player before returning to the original pair. If the ring is thrown back and forth between two people, the ring immediately changes team possession.

❑ During the ten-catch sequence the ring may be caught in any way; grabbing, spearing, trapping, etc.

❑ After catching the ring a player may run as far and long as they like within the boundaries, but if they stop before throwing the ring, they must stay in that spot until the ring is released.

❑ Guarding and blocking shots is allowed, but absolutely no physical contact between players is permitted at any time during the game — except the occasional high-five.

❑ If a goal shot is attempted and dropped (remember it must be speared to count), the other team gets immediate possession.

If no goals are being scored or even attempted, lower the catch sequence requirement from 10 to say 7, or even less if necessary.

To begin play after a score, ask anyone to throw the ring high somewhere near the center of the playing area.

If the boys (or any aggressive, adept individual) are dominating play, reduce use of their dominant hand by putting on a mitten (slip a sliced-off section of panty-hose over both hands). Or tie their legs firmly together — that'll slow 'em down.

INITIATIVE PROBLEMS

Don't we have enough problems without making up more? Well sure, but these are initiative problems — fabricated situations presented by a facilitator who sets the parameters for operation and safety, then steps back and allows the group (team) to attempt a solution. The "problems" are designed to invite a group to come up with a workable solution, but the hidden reasoning involves the dynamics that occur when people are challenged as a group — cooperation, communication, trust and commitment.

There's no doubt that we all have enough problems in our own lives, but being able to work together in a controlled setting to solve a recognized fabrication gives us the tools and experience to better solve the "real" problems.

Don't become so intent on "good stuff" happening that you forget the fun. As the level of enjoyment decreases so does the commitment to participate. Fun is perhaps your most important and most ignored teaching tool; i.e., **Funn Stuff**.

Bored; i.e., Board

Materials needed for this terminally tedious task.

❑ Four — 1" X 10" X 8' boards If you normally deal with smaller groups, the boards only need to be 6 feet long.

After re-reading this write-up, I realized that writing about the activity was more fun than doing it — so I hope you enjoy reading the next few paragraphs.

Here's the part that makes this activity worth doing. After the group is standing on the linearly arranged boards, ask each individual to choose what animal they most relate to and then line up, on the boards, as to the size of that animal. Of course, while achieving that announced zoological configuration, no one is allowed to step off a board into the environmentally noxious layer of whatever your over stimulated imagination has come up with — try dioxin, metamurphix acid, or tri-oxy-putrimiasmic flurodine. If a slip is experienced, penalties are in store. Be somewhat compassionate toward identifying transgressions and application of consequences.

If the animal ploy sounds too anthropomorphic, try lining up by the first three numbers of their social security number. Everybody has one now-a-days (Has a what? A SS # — pay attention!), but if they can't remember, substitute some birthday numbers or their shoe size.

You can also ask the bored students to simply change board ends without stepping off for no reason other than because of the implicit challenge, but that's pretty obvious and boring. (Ever notice how much the word *pretty* is used as an emphasizer? Like, ...that's pretty good, or pretty bad, or pretty hard, etc.

Pretty also acts as a preface to my favorite oxymoron — PRETTY UGLY.)

If your not in a thinking/creative mood, here's a few more "things to do".

- ❏ No talking allowed on the second try.
- ❏ Try to do it faster, and faster, and faster until warp speed is reached.
- ❏ Ask the group to close their eyes or hand out blindfolds.
- ❏ Handicap some or all of the group members by suggesting that they not use an arm or hand.

The crux of all this is that even a potentially boring activity can be made acceptably exciting by an upbeat and innovative presentation. And, it follows, exciting activities can be made wearisome by an uninspired or overly competitive presentation. And that's the truth...

Circle Slap

This is a prone variation (via AP/PA Trainer, Charlie Harrington) of the ole *Knee Slap* activity, where people stand or sit in a circle with their hands on each other's knees. This, of course, causes arms to be crossed, resulting in a modicum of confusion as to whose hand is where. A knee slap is initiated somewhere in the circle's arc and continues sequentially until someone slaps out of sequence — happens all the time. Then you either start over, laugh at the miss-slap and continue, or reverse direction of the slapping.

For *Circle Slap*, your players lie in a circle, ventral-down on the floor with everyone's head oriented toward the center. Arms and hands are further extended toward the center, then crossed over the arms of the person to your right and left — palms down. Check out the photo...

A floor slap is initiated by someone and passed in sequence around the circle of hands. If a double slap is given, the slap sequence reverses. If three slaps are delivered, the slapping person must wink at someone else across the circle,

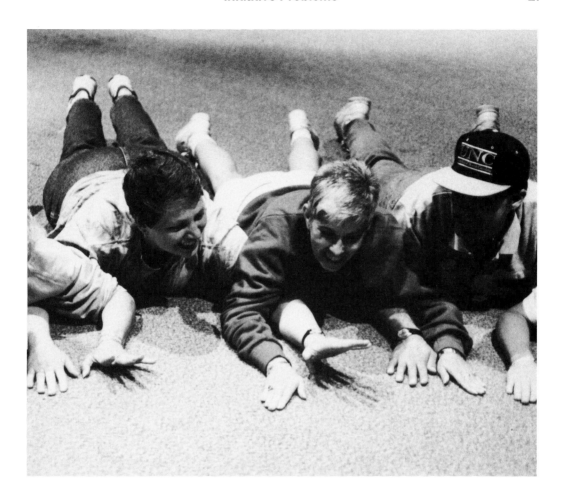

and the receiver responds with a single or double slap, (a double slap sends it back to the winker).

Try starting two slaps using the above rules. Can you handle chaos? Can you handle the dust clouds billowing off the rug?

Human Overhand

When I first thought of the idea for this activity my reaction was, "This is much too easy." After having watched

well over 20 groups struggle to tie a simple overhand knot, with their bodies representing part of the tying rope, I'm ready to say this initiative is a real poser, a stumpfying, conundrumistic puzzle.

The Set Up — Pass out 6' lengths of small diameter rope (*Buddy Ropes*; **QuickSilver**, pg. 220) to six or eight people. Ask them to hold the ropes between them — hand to hand — so that they represent a hand-in-rope line; person, rope, person type thing. Tell the participants to, "...be the rope."

The Problem — Ask the group to try and tie a simple overhand knot in the *center rope* without anyone letting go of their individual grasp of the ropes. Take one of the ropes and illustrate what an overhand knot looks like. Return the rope and BEGIN. (Note: Use a different colored rope section for the center rope.)

If the group imagines that their arms and bodies are an extension of the individual ropes, by carefully maneuvering they should be be able to complete the knot within a few minutes. Doesn't happen! The group regularly underestimates the comitted maneuvering required and overestimates their initial grasp of the problem. Working on this knot can represent a humbling time for a group. Be prepared for a debrief that might cover the following:

❑ How do you handle group frustration?
❑ Why was the solution so illusive?
❑ What was the turning point that allowed your group to finally tie the knot?
❑ If you did not achieve your goal, does that designate a lack of success? What is success in this context?

Hint: *Everyone* on one side of the center rope has to go through that small loop. See photo below.

The Knot!

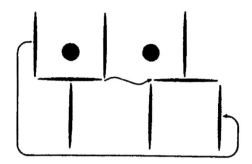 

The Movable Martini   P/2

Many years ago I included the following Old Fashioned cocktail puzzle in an issue of *Bag of Tricks*. It's essentially a combination of toothpicks and a penny so arranged as to look like an Old Fashioned cocktail glass with a cherry immersed. The idea is to move the "cherry" outside the glass (represented by the toothpicks) by manipulating a minimum number of toothpicks. Toothpicks can be moved, the penny cannot. And here's the solution:

I offered the solution so readily here because I had already given it up in that long ago issue, and because this fairly easy conundrum was just a warm up for the following stickler.

Looking at the toothpick martini glass with olive depicted above, what is the minimum number of toothpicks you must move to get the olive outside the martini glass?

Answer: **None**. Turn the paper 121° in either direction. Is that great, or what? I love lateral solutions like that! This variation of the Old Fashioned (hold the cherry) problem is a brain child of Martin Gardner.

The Net

Here's a rainy day puzzler that shouldn't take too long to figure out, but beware, it could be deadly.

Set the simulated scene. You and your buddy are SCUBA diving in the Florida Keys, and are attracted to a sunken ship in about 50' of water. A deck-hold on the recently downed ship is wide open. Knowing that valuable cargo (a trove of Barry Manilow CD's) is there for the taking, you both enter the hold and begin filling your dive bag with discs.

During this time, a Russian trawler passing overhead has dropped a fishing net that becomes entangled with the ship's superstructure and tightly covers the hold opening, your only exit to the surface. With only one minute of air left, you and your partner must determine how to cut through the net so that the least number of net strands are severed. If you cut one more than the minimum, the remainder of the strands will not separate. At the end of one minute you and your partner are allowed to take a deep breath to extend your time. If either one of you exhales and breathes again before the correct number of strands are cut (announced), you both become... anoxic flatliners.

Brainstorming, listening to one another, controlling panic, acting efficiently on ideas. Talk about it.

The "answer" net is also included because some of you smokers just aren't going to make it to the surface without some help.

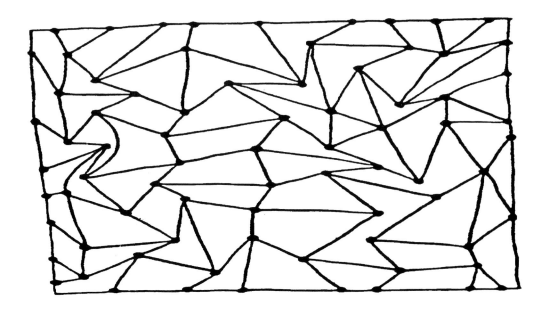

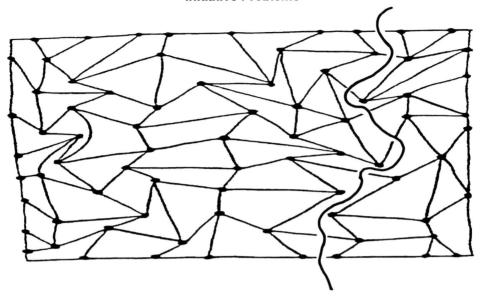

Twirlie Bull's Eye & Twirlie Up Chuck

I'm sure these whirlie things have a commercial name or two or three, but I call them twirlies, because that's what they are. I've played with them occasionally over the years (they always seem to be available at craft fairs for exorbitant prices) but never paid much attention to their play potential until I bought a few at Victoria Market in Melbourne. I'm not sure why I bought them — the price was probably right — but I'm glad that I did because workshop participants love them.

Timing their use is important, and the right time is right away. When people show up for a workshop and are standing around trying to make small talk and not drink a fourth cup of coffee, bring out the twirlies and launch a couple skyward. Seeing how easy it is to use and how visually gratifying their short flights become, hands-on people can't wait to give it a spin, and even the "We cool" folks that hang on the periphery of participation usually give the twirlie a try.

Spinning a few of these IFOs (Identified Flying Objects) towards a self-conscious group of work shop participants gives them something attractive to try until the "real" program starts. Spinning a twirlie isn't "all thrill, no skill", but it's close.

A twirlie is simply a small propellor (plastic or wood) fixed to the end of a six inch long, small diameter dowel. When you spin the dowel rapidly between your palms, the entire device will helicopter it's way up to 25' **IF** you spin the dowel in a counterclockwise direction. Otherwise (clockwise) the spinning propeller will try to eat your knuckles — experiential education at its best.

Using twirlies is kind of like using comet balls, people like them because they like them, but here's something to try after your group tires of just twirlin'.

Gather up your players and explain that you want them all to spin their twirlies up on your count of three, and that you want everyone then to try and catch a descending twirlie, as long as it's not the one they lofted.

If a twirlie hits the floor (remains uncaught), someone must pick it up and hold it overhead so that you can get a count of the ones missed. This total represents the team's negative score. On the next try (coming right up) they will try to reduce their negative score; i.e., the number of twirlies on the floor.

After a few tries, if there's not some improvement, suggest they all get

together and talk about technique or strategize about how they can improve their efforts as a team. Sometimes it's necessary for you, as facilitator, to suggest some form of communication, because most groups are so used to pure recreation (or not-so-pure fooling around) that problem solving is not a priority as long as the fun factor's high.

Don't forget **Twirlie Bull's Eye**! I did and was about to put what I had written above into *save* when I noticed the rubric of this playful piece. No wonder I can never find my glasses, or remember to... what?

With twirlies in hand, ask the group to make a circle around the center jump circle on a basketball court. (If you don't have a basketball court consider yourself lucky — you don't have to listen to that incessant ball/floor contact noise. To substitute, make two concentric circles that duplicate the basketball set up, using tape, chalk or a section of rope.) The outer people circle should have a radius of about 20'.

Objective

To spin all the twirlies into the inner circle as quickly and efficiently as possible; this is a timed event. Mention that a minimum of two attempts are planned so that a team can plan to try and better their first effort.

Rules

❏ After the first spin on GO, the twirlie can be picked up (by anyone) from where it lands and spun again.

❏ Each twirlie must end up completely within the inner circle. If even a fraction of its blade or turning dowel is on the line, it must be retrieved and spun again.

❏ It is not necessary for each player to have a twirlie at the start.

❏ A player cannot jump into the center circle because that area is pressure sensitive and anything over 8 ounces will set off an explosive device. Go ahead and try, but I told you so.

❏ The outside circle is coated with an insidiously noxious substance that cannot be touched. If a player is so careless as to make corporal contact with this area while trying to retrieve a twirlie, a five second penalty is loudly announced.

❏ A twirlie-in-hand cannot be used to rake other twirlies from this taboo area.

❏ twirlies must be spun into the inner circle, not simply tossed.

❏ The clock stops when the final twirlie comes to rest completely within the inner circle.

Talk about — teamwork, people establishing what they do best, following rules to establish the challenge, "failing forward", communicating about what needs to be done to improve.

If you ask all the players in the circle to sit down before spinning their twirlie, you could call this activity *Sit and Spin*.

Sequences

When I run into a cerebral problem (usually written) it better have an attractive solution (a head slapper) or it's off my conceptual list. The following three sequence puzzles bowled me over, but I liked the answers enough to pass them along to you. Use them as part of your *Mastermind* list of presentation ponderables.

What is the pattern that makes the following number sequence logical?

8 5 4 9 1 7 6 3 2 0

Answer: The numbers are in *alphabetical order*. Is that great...? Numbers in alphabetical order... what a neatly skewed notion.

****

With a twist of thinking, re-skew your notions with the following letter line.

O T T F F S S

What is the next letter in this sequence? Hint: To reach the end of this letter line will take more time than you've got.

Answer: The next letter is E and the sequence is infinite. These letters are in *numerical order*. Oh Wow! How could I have missed that? Beats me!

****

Check out this series of symbols or what appears to be letters of an ancient exotic language. There is a definite pattern established by these 7 symbols which suggests an infinite progression. What is the next symbol after the triangle?

↑ ⋉ 8 ⯊ ⯂ ⯎ ▽ 88 etc.

Take a ruler and using the straight edge vertically divide each of the symbols exactly in half. What's left? or right in this case! "... 7, 8 lay 'em straight; 9, 10 big fat hen."

Zits and a *NEAT Variation

Lest you think that **ZITS** is an acronym for **Z**any **I**nitials **T**arget **S**illiness, be aware that these initiative simile situations are like... representative of solid on-going scientific research. Which is to say that the letters **ZITS** represent distinct areas of epidermal infection caused by a chemical imbalance within the body. The metaphorical purpose of solving the initiative aspect of this problem is to neutralize the chemical imbalance and eliminate those purulent pustules.

Having discretely handled that ubiquitous social stigma, here's the scoop on another useful swinging initiative. Credit the idea for this IP to the folks at *Project Adventure Australia* who are so chemically in-balance that **ZITS** has become **ALOE** (**A**ustralian **L**aughter **O**vercomes **E**rysipelas) — and thank goodness for that.

What you need

❑ A medical dictionary to look up *erysipelas*.
❑ A standard Nitro Crossing-type swing rope.
❑ Numbered gym spots to equal the number of participants. Use the gym spots that have already been num-

bered for the initiative problem, *Key Punch*.

Procedure

The discs need to be numbered sequentially on the underside (recognizing that the reverse side also has a reverse side), and randomly distributed in an unmarked circle. At the center of this nebulous circular area is the suspended swing rope.

The spots should be placed far enough apart so that stepping from one to another is tempting but not possible. If arranging the spots causes the rope to arc-out more than three metres from plumb, then you have too many players; remove a few of the far-out spots.

Ask the group to number-off and then choose any spot to stand on, (the spot numbers are underneath). Remind each player to remember their assigned number, and then check their spot number. This will ascertain the level of chemical imbalance that must be homeopathically treated—in this case by minimal corporal movement.

The task is to right the chemical imbalance by relocating players so that the spot on which they are standing corresponds with their assigned number: you gotta' end up standing on a matching number.

The area around the spots represents many of the likely causes of this chemi-

---

* If you wondered, the rubric **NEAT** is an acronym for **N**o **E**xercise **A**ll **T**alk.

cal imbalance and *must* be avoided. The swing rope (with the Clearasil label prominently affixed) represents the most obvious solution prop.

Each spot can support no more than two feet at any time. If a spot is touched simultaneously by more than two feet, or if a player touches down inside the purulent area, the "domino principal" penalty is brought into play. The offender must return to their original spot, and if someone else has since located on that spot, they too must return to their original spot, etc.

If a penalty is incurred, the Clearasil rope is returned to the centre of the circle.

This activity can be used to:

❑ subversively build upper body strength.
❑ build team affiliation and camaraderie in a speed mode.
❑ allow a group to work through the cooperation and communication problems that will invariably result as the participants work toward a joint solution.
❑ provide some programmatic fun.

If you don't have a rope, try this U.K. variation.

NEAT Puzzle

David Wheatley from Cumbria sent this "...exercise that you may have seen that we have adapted a little." No worries David, adapting is an occupational way of life, and we already played a very similar game above using a rope.

(parenthetical inserts represent editorial comments.)

"Nine discs (use gym spots, like in *Key Punch* or *Frog Wars*) are set out in a 3′ X 3′ grid on the floor. Each disc has a number from 1-9 on the bottom, and the numbers are randomly set within the grid.

A group of eight each stands on a disc. Each person also has an assigned number (known to everyone) from one to eight.

The task is for the group to arrange themselves on a disc of corresponding number. (If I'm a 3, I need to be standing on disc #3.)

Rules:

❑ Only a disc that is not being stood on can be turned and read.
❑ Only one person can stand on a disc at one time.
❑ Two moves may not be made simultaneously.
❑ Players can only move linearly, not diagonally.

Hint: If the groups work out the sequence around the outside of the grid, they can then arrange themselves using the center disc to slip people in and out

of the sequence. Once on the center disc
they merely rotate until they think they
are on the correct disc."

TRUST

I'm talkin' about physical and emotional trust here. *Is my belay going to work? Will I be safe? Are you going to make fun of me? Can I offer something if it's not what you want to hear? Am I going to get hurt?* Without it your group may get started, but the in between will be blah and the end may come sooner than you anticipated.

Consistently work on building trust. Your students (whatever age), because of societal pressures to succeed, have been indirectly taught not to trust. *Trust? Yeah, it sounds good, but risky. Get 'em before they get you, I'd say. Stay on top, don't give 'em an advantage.* This is not funny, but represents an attitute that's all too prevalent. Trust in the context of adventure programming is absolutely integral to cooperation and team building.

Co-op Competition

This is a body orientation variation of an activity that's on page 5 of **The Bottomless Bag Again!?**, and was passed along during a recent American Camping Association convention in Chicago by a woman with light brown hair (modified page-boy as I remember), about 5'4", wearing a pair of commercially faded blue jeans and a pleasant smile. Thank you anonymous lady.

In the past, I always presented this up-close-and-personal cooperative exercise by suggesting that the two participants stand facing one another, making contact *only* with their toes and palms of their hands. By requesting this I was positioning the partners so that they were at the same time close, but required to maintain a working distance from one another.

The insightful workshop woman mentioned above, suggested that the two participants continue to stand vis-à-vis, but this time with one foot forward and one foot back. If you try this you'll notice that the foot and hand contact is identical (unselfconscious touch) but that the duo now has considerably more room to maneuver than if they were squared off, face-to-face.

This is ostensibly a stretching exercise, but the subtle rationale includes cooperating and competing at the same time. Stop reading, try it!

First Names Only

"The sweetest sound in the world is your own name." That old saying isn't meant to promote egoism, just stating a basic truism. People like to hear and see their own name, so here's a chance for them to do that.

Ask someone in your group (class) who has a comparatively long first name (like Jennifer — not Sue) to print their name on the chalkboard (butcher paper). Then someone else can volunteer to be next, using one of the letters in JENNIFER as one of the letters in their name. Soon, the arrangement of the names begins to look like a well contested scrabble game or a crossword puzzle.

When completed, the name of each individual in the group is displayed and interconnected. Leave the names exhibited for a period of time so that the students can take pride in their role as a member of the group (team) and for the inherent joy of just seeing their name interconnected with others.

Isn't that simple? If this is the second time you have read this, how come you haven't tried it? Just a reminder, 'cause you're so busy, and all...

Have You Ever...

If you have perused **The Bottomless Bag Again!?** or more recently **QuickSilver** you know my penchant for collecting and recording unique experiences revealed in the guise of a question, *Have you ever...?* Well, have you ever...

...plunged into a pool from a 3 meter diving board in a kayak?

...free rappelled over 100 feet into a cave and used mechanical ascenders to climb the same rope?

...competed in a sanctioned dart tournament?

...purposefully painted over rust to hide it?

...dived on The Great Barrier Reef in Australia?

...struck your hand purposefully into the open maw of a living giant clam?

...seen the Aurora Borealis?

...mushed a multi-dog sled team?

...been served a *special* meal on a commercial airline?

...been paid in gold for having performed a job?

...physically "set foot" in all 50 of the United States?

...been accused of plagiarizing yourself?

...touched the Alaskan Pipe Line?

...purposefully killed an animal larger than yourself?

...bought someone a present at your local discount store and put it into a Saks Fifth Ave box?

...served something frightfully fattening to someone on a diet and swear to that person it only has 20 calories?

...led an indoor hands-on play session with over 250 people?

...boot skied?

...kept your eyes open during a sneeze?

...walked *at least* half-a-mile on a rail road track without falling off?

...snapped an all leather bull whip?

...eaten hot boiled peanuts?

...sat in a hot tub and had the hair on your head (what's left of it) freeze?

...been the best man at your 86 year old father's wedding? (This one's for you Pop!)

I answered yes to 19 of these 24 questions. How about you? I know... I know... it's my test and I made up the questions. OK, send me *your* test and we'll compare.

If you are using these type of questions programmatically, however, don't compare, just use them as a benign prod toward gaining more experience and for sharing what the folks in your group have done.

Keystone or I Lean

Jim Schoel laid this simple but intense activity on me. He also dreamed up both names, and they both fit fine, but *I Lean* makes me smile.

Make a shoulder-to-shoulder circle with 5-7 people. The object is to main-

tain that *shoulder contact* as you ask the group to lean in toward the center of the circle, concurrently moving their feet away from circle center. The participants are not allowed to use their hands or arms to support themselves on one

another, but must try to arrange their bodies in juxtaposition to one another so that each person represents a "keystone", holding the group together as the lean continues and becomes more challenging.

The group will know when they are leaning at maximum. After maintaining a balanced posture for about five seconds, ask them to look up and make eye contact with the other keystoners. This invariably causes smiles that escalate to laughs, resulting in a happy disintigration of the leaning tower of extra cheese pizza.

Bring up the concept of what makes a keystone so important in bridge or arch building. If possible have a picture or illustration available. Make the comparison between an architectural keystone and what each leaning body represents in the circle, and correspondingly what each individual means to the support of the group.

Hint — I've found, while role playing a keystone, that I get a better lean and more support from my two partners if I put the back of my hands on my lower back/hip area (hands about 6-8 inches apart) with my elbows akimbo.

Mangle

After fooling around with **Keystone**, try this gauntlet-type activity for some uninhibited unselfconscious full body contact mingling. Come on... don't stop thinking about it just because of my warped sense of corporal contact;

Mangle can be fun. Be sure to sequence correctly, however. This is not a first day, get to know you, low key game.

Do you remember what a *mangle* is or was? If you're over 50 there's a good chance your grandmother used one for pressing clothes. There was also a mangle used for squeezing the water out clothes after being tub washed. Both mangles consisted of two cylinders that were placed together and rotated in opposite directions under pressure.

So, why not try a human mangle? Exactly what I was thinking. In fact, I've already done a few, so let me suggest a beginning. Mangles have a way of becoming something else as the rotation begins, but that lends itself to creativity and responding to challenge — just what the administration has been asking for. Is this fortuitous serendipity, or what?

Ask pairs (about the same height works best ...and maintains the mangle's warranty) to stand shoulder to shoulder facing you in a column of two (two lines of people). The pair standing behind the first pair (front to back), and on down the line, should be within 12" of one another; i.e., close.

Ask for two volunteers (approx. same height and temperament) to enter the

mangle. The mangle begins operating as the first pair, maintaining constant contact with one another, (manglers should keep their arms at their sides) begin rotating respectively in opposite directions. The rotation should be such so that the people to be mangled are drawn (sucked) into the line of pairs. All the in-line pairs should now be rotating identically with the first pair, as the mangled volunteer pair is twisted and mass massaged to the end of the mangle line.

Ejected by the last rotating pair, the well-touched dyad take their place in line as manglers rather than manglees. The first pair then allows themselves to be drawn into the mangle (enter laterally rather than head on; it's easier to get "sucked in' with a sideways orientation) and the twisting, turning, bumping, laughing, warming constant-contact continues, until lunch or someone lets one.

Run! Shout! Knock Yourself Out

This is really simple. If you don't get this on the first read through, you are being entirely too serious or suffering from profound alexia.

Locate your group at one end of a loong field. (The longest playing field I've ever been on was an Australian-Rules Footy Pitch in Tasmania. Wait...

that might not be true. I walked on a polo field once in Wenham, MA — but that's comparing horses and people. Get serious! Other possible venues: a beach, Wal-Mart parking lot on Sunday, any recently reconstituted strip-mining site, Nebraska.)

Indicate that you would like each individual to challenge themselves by simultaneously running and yelling as far and as loud as they can on one lung full of air. When the yelling stops (air's gone), that's their PR (personal record). This activity can be pursued one at a time, so each person has their "run in the sun", or the entire group can cacophonize their way down the field together. Either way, each individual gets to challenge themselves to the level they choose, and you get to present another zany activity that further enhances your established off-the-wall reputation as — that teacher who doesn't teach, but we sure learn a lot.

❑ To down-play who "gets the furthest...", allow the participants to run in any direction they choose.
❑ See if any of the players would like to try this activity as a pair. Taking off hand-in-hand, they can either yell together or, to increase their Doppler effect, attempt the run as a tag team.
❑ Encourage team cheering for whatever attempt is made by an individual.

I'm confident that yelling for distance will not become a varsity sport, so remember not to encourage practicing.

I observed Donné Frisson (PA trainer from Nova Scotia) presenting this activity during an Adventure Programming workshop. Donné, how come you stopped so soon?

Subway Sardines

This bit of chaos comes with a caveat: don't present this activity to your group until you are convinced that they can handle the responsible attitude necessary to keep people from getting bumped around. This gentle but sincere warning provides a further reminder and reinforcement of the fact that *sequencing of activities* is an integral part of adventure programming.

Ask your confident and compassionate group, (See, I'm convinced you're ready) to circle up so that each person is at least 25 feet from the center of the circle. Request that everyone assume the *bumpers-up* * position. If you don't know what a bumpers-up position is, don't continue with this exercise until you read below.

Indicate that on command, everyone will walk slowly toward the center of the circle and, corporal contact notwithstanding, continue walking to the far side of the circle.

The object of this request is to cause incidental contact as everyone meets at circle-center, but to handle this contact in such a way that each person feels comfortable squeezing and gently bumping past one another. Add to the developing good humor by suggesting that each person politely indicate, "Excuse me", "Pardon me" at each contact.

---

*bumpers up — A protect-yourself posture taken by someone who is about to move about with their eyes closed. The position is assumed by holding your arms in front of the body, elbows bent and directly ventral to the torso, hands at face level, palms forward, (see photo). This "bumpers" positioning is primarily for facial protection so don't separate your hands to the side of the face.

Congratulate all for making the passage in such good form, then ask them to repeat the trip, but this time to walk a bit faster. If the first trip through was a disaster, don't ask them to repeat their mistakes without some discussion. If the second attempt demonstrates a continued lack of control, switch to another less intimidating activity.

If all's well, ask the group to attempt a slow jog through circle-center. And finally, to attempt the passage at a slow walk with their *eyes closed*.

The rationale behind this potentially frightening activity is to build trust, but also to demonstrate to the group how far they have progressed (via participation in other trust activities) toward caring more about each other's physical welfare than the importance of reaching an announced goal.

Being able to consistently *Go For It*, also requires that you be able to occasionally *Stop For It*.

War Lock

This is a one-on-one game that works best with a group that has already established a level of playfulness amongst one another, or with a group that is obviously ready to play. If you are in doubt as to a group's readiness, try a quick round of *Your Add* (**Bottomless Bag Again !?**; pg. 48) to test their responsiveness.

Someone initiates the game by establishing eye contact with someone else (for whatever reason or no reason) and says "LOCK". When the other person hears that word, and decides to accept the ocular challenge, they must concentrate on not losing eye contact as they reply convincingly "DOUBLE LOCK". The contest is on. The first person to break eye contact loses that particular match.

If a person hears LOCK, and decides eyeball jousting isn't their thing, that individual must cast their eyes downward, and mutter "BUC-BUC"; a fowl sound indeed. The predatory initiator, recognizing that their potential prey has little sense of aqueous humor, must then move on to another innocent set of limpid pools.

However, if the match is on, each player tries to make the other person lose eye contact. Moving, gesticulating, head bobbing and sticking out your tongue are all allowed, but no physical contact is permitted.

As a game ploy to cause breaking eye contact, players can show a chosen number of extended fingers (see photo),

trying to perform this digital display at the periphery of the opposing player's vision. Both players can thus gesticulate madly, but if an incorrect number of fingers is guessed, the erring guesser loses the match, a correct guess wins. Guessing or displaying fingers is not mandatory, but once a sequence of fingers is flashed the number cannot be changed.

The person who is challenged, after having accepted the challenge, gets to choose the length of the contest. The initiator, after having heard DOUBLOCK, asks "TIME?" The person being challenged can say either "GO FOR IT" or "MILLENNIUM". A *GO FOR IT* contest lasts approximately one minute and can end in a tie; a *MILLENNIUM* commitment drags on inevitably to a win/loss.

I'll take a GO FOR IT anytime, how about you? BUC BUC?

Yeah Teachers!

Here's a test for teachers. Ice breaking? Camaraderie? Team Building? Right!

Categories	**Guidelines**	**Bonus Points**
•Teaching Time:	A point for each full year teaching in a public school	5 pts if you left and returned to teaching after working in some other profession
•Grades:	A point for each separate grade taught (1 full year)	20 pts if you taught ten or more years
•Traveler:	A point for each state that you have taught in (1 full year)	5 pts for teaching out of the US (1 month min.)
•Recognition:	A point for each local award received	15 pts for national recognition
•Language:	A point for each language taught	5 pts for fluency
•Family:	A point for each close family relation who is/was a teacher	5 pts if you are a child or parent of a teacher
•Contribution:	A point for each article published regarding education or a media interview on the subject	10 pts if distributed nationally
•Diversity:	A point for each hobby practiced weekly	5 pts if its used regularly in your teaching
•Membership:	A point for each professional educational association to which you belong	5 pts if you belong to less than three
•Memories:	A point for each piece of memorabilia you currently have on you that relates to a teaching experience	10 pts if you are wearing bell bottoms or polyester
•Laughter:	A point if you laugh at least once during an average work day	5 pts for laughing so hard you needed to excuse yourself from class

TEAM TOTAL POINTS_____

Zipper Trust Fall Start

Here's a challenge for a jaded zipper, (remember... it takes a big zipper to make an elephant fly). Rather than standing or sitting or clipping in the Studebaker Wrap from behind, or whatever variations you have been using for second and third trips down the zip wire, ask a multiple ride participant to try the TRUST FALL START.

Clip the pulley rope into the rider's harness or "stud" wrap in front, the same way you would clip them in for a regular zip trip. Ask the participant (once on the platform and clipped in ready to ride) to face the tree or pole, putting their back toward the final destination. The object is to do a regulation trust fall off the edge of the platform. This can only be accomplished on those zips that are set up for a standing start; i.e., with the zip cable far enough above so that head contact cannot be made with the cable from a standing position.

The rider falls backward with hands clasped, attempting not to reach up and grab the pulley rope; a daunting commitment when you consider that as the fall begins the pulley begins to roll down-cable resulting in a much longer fall (slide) than the rider anticipates.

This challenge is not presented as a scare ploy, (tell the rider what to anticipate) or as an opportunity to "hot dog", but is offered as a *Challenge By Choice* option to those participants who want or need an additional challenge.

VARIATIONS

A good game or initiative problem can probably be changed for the better. Don't hesitate to mess with the rules, (remember, no one owns these games). Take a chance. If a new rule doesn't work, drop it — the original game is still intact, and "If it's worth doing, it's worth overdoing." Here's a few outta sight variations to prove my point.

Bugs in my Cup

Hold a coffee cup in your hands and ask an attentive group, "How many bugs are there in this cup?" The answer, of course, is eight.

Only the rare perceptive player will come up with that definite answer, in fact when you say, "How many bugs was that?" and the answer is five, you can be assured of either a lucky guess or *knowing* about bug numbers.

Finally, when you ask, "How Many?", and the excited voices relay in unison,

"two!", you know that everyone is copacetic, in tune, and synergistically vibrating.

How many words were in each question above? Oh Wow... that's so simple! Hmmmm.

Thanks to Sue Schaefer for not keeping me in the dark about bugs and such.

Clock Rope

Mary Ladd Smith and I developed the initiative problem *The Clock* (**Silver Bullets**; pg. 116) at The Houlton-Richmond School in Danvers, MA; c 1973.

From that **Silver Bullets** write up... "This activity is an example of how a well known child's pastime (Ring-Around-The-Rosie) can be adapted and embellished to produce a challenging initiative problem." Did you know that the game Ring-Around-The-Rosie represents a macabre symbolism of the Bubonic Plague?

To wit:

❑ "Ring around the rosie..." refers to a red rosette marking on the skin that was a precursor of the disease.
❑ "Pocket full of posies..." indicates the fragrant small flowers that were kept close at hand to hide the overwhelming stench of unburied decaying bodies.
❑ "Ashes, ashes..." was actually "Aachoo, Aachoo..." sneezing was another manifestation of the disease.

❑ "All fall down..." everyone dies!!!

Cute little ditty from the brothers Grimm.

Decimation and death aside, here's a usable variation of the normal hand-in-hand circling technique. Use your YURT rope (**QuickSilver**, pg. 258) to hold as the players make their double rotation around the 12-3-6-9 o'clock markers within the people circle. Use of the rope precludes having to hold hands and makes the rotation seem more enjoyable.

Afterwards, as you sit with your group debriefing the activity, notice how most of the participants continue to hold onto the rope, using it's supple strength as an unconscious metaphoric link with the other players. Am I stretching? Not this time. This is not my normal tongue-in-cheek reaction to overblown results, the rope actually does seem to be a meaningful connector. Don't take it away...

Group Juggle Variations

The activity, *Group Juggle* has been around for a number of years and is usually played in association with the initiative problem *Warp Speed*. Both of those activities are detailed in **The Bottomless Bag Again !?**

Try these variations

❏ Each person adopts a sound, then whenever they throw a ball in the juggle sequence they loudly proclaim that sound.

❏ Call out REVERSE as soon as most balls are in play. The group will probably fumble around, drop most of the balls and good-naturedly complain. The object is to switch direction of the throwing sequence without a dropped ball. Try again.

❏ Using only 2-4 balls (per group of 12), try starting 2 balls in one direction and 2 balls in the reverse direction. It's difficult to complete even one round, but it can be done.

❏ Add a distinctly shaped or colored ball as a "rumor" which, as you know, can move anywhere and usually at blinding speed.

❏ Substitute small water balloons for balls — on a warm day!

❏ Try completing this exercise using Iky-Poo balls or GAK.

❏ Play this game with a raw egg or two thrown in as a consequence.

Name Tag Variation

I just tried looking up the game, **Name Tag**, so I could refer to it as previously presented in *Bag of Tricks*, or in a Project Adventure publication, but I can't find it. Did I ever write about it? I'm not sure, but after just spending longer than I wanted to looking through electronic files for whatever it was that I think I said (wrote — same thing), I figure that I'm better off just writing what's currently on my mind. Maybe I'll find *Name Tag* later on, and if so, you will never read this — but you are, so I didn't.

Rather than continuing my *mouse hunt*, here are the basic rules—so I can tell you about a variation that Lee Gillis (National Trainer and Psychology Professor at Georgia College) passed along. This all seems a bit circuitous, but the game and the variation are worthwhile.

Name Tag is a name-reminder game, so the group would have had to previously play one of the other games that associates faces and names.

Ask the group to close their eyes and with "bumpers up" (hands protecting faces) to slowly mill around until you say, "Stop". When the group is nicely separated (you may have to ask them to mill away from one another) and spatially disoriented, tell them that you are going to tap somebody's shoulder and say aloud that person's name. The tapped person immediately opens her/his eyes and quickly finds someone nearby to tap and name. This procedure continues until everyone has had a turn.

As a convenience to the tapped and often frantically searching player, each person who has had a turn should kneel or sit down to indicate that their tag turn is complete.

Tell the group before you begin that their attempt from start to finish will be timed. Try this activity at least twice so that the group gets the opportunity to best their previous time, and hopefully allows forgetful folks (like me) to wet-cement a couple more names in place.

It's embarrassingly interesting to watch a tapped player open his/her eyes, look directly at the person in front of them, then dash off to tag someone at a distance. It's painfully obvious why the vis-á-vis person is ignored, but the forgetting and enjoyment of the consequence is shared, as names eventually become people.

Variation (Finally) — When a person taps someone and says their name, rather than continuing individually, that pair must join hands and attach themselves to a third person, etc., etc. The game ends (stop the watch) when everyone has joined hands. In a circle? Straight line, semi-circle, egg shape, ...whatever.

Was it worth it? Well, I guess! **NAME TAG! NAME TAG! — YES! YES!! YES!!!**

TP Shuffle Variation —The TP Sprint

If you're interested, refer to **The Bottomless Bag**; pg. 243, or **Silver Bullets**; pg. 110 for the original presentations.

Rather than splitting the group in half, and asking the log-mounted individuals to change ends without touching the ground, add some variety by asking the log- riders to:

❏ ...choose a standing place on the log as to their respective ages, youngest to oldest, etc. Then ask the players to reverse their positions on the log as to their chronologic ages. The answer to any question you or the students have about this is *yes*.

❏ ...ask the students to line up on the log so that the most height impaired person is at one end and the tallest individual is at the other end. Switch!

Don't forget *The TP Sprint*! You forgot? It's on page 91 in **The Bottom-less Baggie**. You don't have the book? Sorry it's out of print. OK ...ok, here's the rules. Place four volunteer "facilita-tors" on the TP log. During the course of the problem they are not allowed to step off the log.

Split the remainder of the team in half. Each half moves separately to either end of the log. Just walk on the grass to the end of the log — we want to finish this by dinner time.

The object is to trade ends of the log as quickly and efficiently as possible, recognizing that the starting and ending positions for each team (same team really) is standing on the ground at the respective ends of the log. Place a short length of slash rope perpendicular to each end of the log. That's the start and finish line you are not allowed to step over and/or into the toxic material—which looks like dirt and grass to most people.

Rules and Penalties

❏ The four facilitators must maintain individual contact with the log. If any of the four inadvertently or purposefully slip off the log, each ground touch receives a 30 second penalty.

❑ This 30 second penalty for each trip to the turf also holds for all other participants.

❑ No props are allowed to be used.

❑ If a devious group figures out that touching the ground and taking the penalty is more efficient than playing it straight, invoke the travesty rule, which in part states, *"To maintain the integrity of the game as stated in the initial rules, and to protect against outlandish (sneaky) initiative machina-* *tions, the instructor may, without warning, change the extent and/or duration of incurred penalties as to best maintain the original intent of the gaming situation."*

There are a couple beautiful solutions to this variation, and I'm not going to tell you what they are because your groups will eventually show you, and one of them is depicted in the photo above.

Rasta Balls

Comet Ball fans will like this.

Having trouble finding ladies' knee-highs at the right price? (That's probably redundant; do they make men's knee-highs?) Feel funny about taking 6 dozen multi-hued knee highs up to the check-out counter? Try making up a few *Rasta Balls* and see how they throw; I think you'll like the comparison.

You already know that Comet Balls are well received as play objects, (Ref. **Bottomless Bag Again!?** - pg. 68; or **Silver Bullets** - pg. 25) so don't look for reasons not to make up a couple Rasta Balls. Here's how.

Using a sharp knife with a pointed, *lock-back* type blade (so that you don't inadvertently close the blade on your finger, which is easy to do when puncturing tennis balls) make a change-purse type slice in the tennis ball, just large enough (1.25" at the most) to push an overhand knot into.

Cut a 4' length of 1/4" polypropylene rope, tie an overhand knot in one end, and force that knot into the sliced ball. (If the knot easily enters the slice, it will also easily exit. Make another smaller slice into the ball and *push* that knotted sucker in there.) Either let the entire

length of rope exiting the ball fray (cowstail) to produce a *Whole Rasta* or tape the rope about halfway from the rope end to the ball and let it fray to the tape: a *Half Rasta*. The availability of Quarter Rastas is obviously there, but remember, the less fray the more speed. Quarter Rasta balls are for experienced catchers only.

Rasta/Comet Ball Comparison

Rasta

- ❏ Inexpensive (4 feet of 1/4" poly rope is cheaper than one Queen-size knee-high)
- ❏ Doesn't fly as far
- ❏ Easier to catch — see Quarter Rasta caveat above
- ❏ More time spent fabricating (slicing rope and shoving knots into 30 balls is no fun)
- ❏ More visual; looks like a toy

Comet

❑ Slightly higher and longer flight path (depends somewhat on who's throwing)

❑ Proper knee-highs are harder to come by

❑ More initial resistance to use (knee highs look like what they are)

❑ More satisfying to throw for the power thrower (has to do with the knee-high's elasticity)

❑ Easier to put together

❑ Knee highs can be used to put over your head for the game *Cranial Snatch It*

If you cut a 3' length of 1/4" bungee cord and use that in place of the poly rope, the spin and release sequence becomes even more problematical. I think you will be pleased by the swish/snap sound that results on release.

DO NOT try to catch a bungee cord Comet Ball. The bungee WILL wrap around your forearm, simultaneously snapping some portion of your flesh; resulting in a surprising amount of pain, a livid stripe on your arm, and a reduced inclination to throw another one.

Puzzle Variation

PA trainers, for the last couple years, have been using a macro 15 piece puzzle as part of their training bag of tricks. The object is to provide the puzzle pieces to a blindfolded workshop group, then ask them to assemble the puzzle as efficiently as possible.

The finished puzzle measures 3' X 5' and is fashioned of 1/4" plywood. Functionally it works best to cover each side of the puzzle with a different tactile surface (smooth paint, rough paint) to reduce confusion as to which side of the puzzle is being solved. The configuration of the puzzle pieces is up to you. Take a look at a store-bought puzzle to get pattern ideas. Keep it simple. Fifteen large pieces can take over an hour to put together.

Topics of team work, leadership, cooperation, trust, communication and creativity are all nicely hit upon at some point during the attempt. I obtained the original puzzle idea and complementary puzzle from a teacher and camp operator in Indiana — Caesar Soete.

I recently heard of another puzzle-like scenario that would duplicate the training topics mentioned above. This quirky time-warp presentation will nostalgically appeal to most of the players in your group.

Simply pass out the parts of a Mr. Potato Head (11 pieces) toy-set to a blindfolded group with the same solution intent as the puzzle problem above. Mrs. Potato Head has 13 parts for a larger group attempt and, of course, a tougher solution.

Credit Joel Cryer of *The Corporate Challenge* in Austin, TX with this playful variation.

ROPES COURSE CONSTRUCTION AND IMPLEMENTATION

The following suggestion may sound like heresy coming from an old time ropes course builder, but... spend your budget $$$ on games, props, and initiative scenarios before you think about purchasing a ropes course. There is a lot more of what you are looking for (should be looking for) within an adventure program by utilizing the "low stuff" than by spending big bucks on a high profile ropes course facility. High ropes provide the pizzaz and culminating series of activities that generate poignant and unforgettable memories, but low level games and initiatives are "where it's at" toward developing your stated curriculum goals.

AC/DC — Ascent/Descent

I recently watched a movie called *Medicine Man*, starring Sean Connery. It was about a reclusive curmudgeon-type guy living in a tropical rain forest somewhere who inadvertently discovers the cure for cancer, then can't figure out where the curative substance came from. As improbable as the plot becomes, he and his co-star (attractive and feisty heroine type) spend some *high* time (100+ feet) in the jungle canopy looking for protoplasmic miracle gunk. (It's certainly not going to add to the film's excitement if their lost substance-search involves grubbing around the tree's root system.)

To reach the canopy level, Sean and companion used a counterbalanced rope and pulley system to ascend, precluding what looked like a horrendous climb. It was simply a matter of clip in and go. (I noticed that the film director did a lot of cut shots of the ascent/descent to make it look efficient and acceptably risky. Some of their pulley arrangements just wouldn't work in real life, but, Hey, it's a movie. As Gloree would say at home, "...if you're going to ruin the movie with facts, go watch football.")

As the result of watching their cinematic penduluming about, I wondered if ascending and descending in a real working situation could be accomplished by climbers counterbalancing one another; i.e, a person descends via gravity on a rope that is reeved through an overhead pulley as another person attached to the same rope is pulled up by that descending person's weight and momentum. More succinctly, as one person comes down, the other person goes up — on the same rope. Obviously thoughts about friction, platform positioning, participant's comparative weight differentials and safety lines needed to be addressed because, "this ain't no movie." So I thought a thought, tried it, and here's the result; a ropes course event called **The AC/DC** — which obviously stands for Ascent/Descent

So far, I have installed two AC/DC's outdoors and two indoors. Indoor installation is predictably easier. To build an AC/DC in trees requires that you spend time looking for just the right orientation of usable limbs or support trunks, whereas the predictable juxtaposing of indoor support beams allows a wider choice of installation positioning.

Operation of the completed event is comparatively easy. One participant climbs on belay to an installed platform. (Outdoors the platform would be installed on the support tree trunk, indoors the platform is wall supported.) That student clips into a length of

available 12mm KM 111 static rope. This section of static rope continues from the student to an overhead pulley (bolted and secured with a rapid link to a beam or limb). The rope continues horizontally from that pulley to an identical second pulley, installed on another support limb or beam, (pulleys are on separate trees). Reeved through the second pulley, the KM 111 rope descends to the ground past a second platform. Climber #2, on the ground, ties or clips into that rope. When climber #1 steps off the platform, climber #2 ascends to his/her platform.

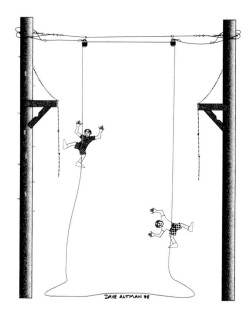

DAVE ALTMAN 95

Details and safety considerations

❏ Installation must be such so that when a climber ascends to a platform that the path of the rope allows the climber to be pulled up and above the platform, not into the bottom of the platform. This is a function of where the overhead pulley is positioned. A 6-8' dangling grab rope may be necessary to allow the ascending and rotating participant to maneuver themselves onto the platform.

❏ If the climbers are approximately equal in weight, the up/down exchange will not happen. The descending climber must be heavier (use a bearing pulley rather than a bushing pulley to reduce friction) to make trading places functional. Thirty-five to forty pounds of weight differential is about right.

I think the following is obvious, but... If the descending climber is too heavy, the ascending climber will accelerate too fast. At the extreme, the person coming down will hit the ground hard and the ascending person might also "hit" something on the way up. Either way, the trust level for future high ropes participation will be substantially diminished. Indulge yourself in the imagined Wylie Coyote scenario, then don't let it happen.

❏ Attach a tag line (1/2" multiline) to the ascending and descending person's harness. If the descending person is coming down too fast, apply tension to the ascending person's tag line. If the descending person is too light, pull down on that person's tag line. Try to arrange weight differentials so that there is no more than a 50 pound differential between climbers. The people who control the tag lines control the safety of this event. If you are the tag line person, *wear gloves*.

❏ Make sure that Climber #1 does not remove their belay rope until Climber #2 has been secured to the AC/DC KM 111 rope. The sequence is this: Climber #1 climbs on belay to the platform, clips into the KM 111 rope and waits. Climber #2 on the ground also clips into the KM 111 rope and announces having done that to Climber #1. Climber #1 acknowledges, then unclips from the belay rope. THIS **MUST** BE DONE **EVERY** TIME THE BELAY ROPE IS USED.

❏ When you install the two overhead pulleys, orient the nut eye bolt anchors so that, when attached, the pulleys will be oriented to allow the static rope to run fairly over the sheave.

❏ Once the up/down sequence is established, no more climbing is necessary. The last person on the platform is lowered to the ground using the initial belay rope.

❏ Of the AC/DC events installed so far, the greatest linear distance between platforms has been about 50'.

Yes, without unclipping, climbers can see-saw up and down until their tag line people get bored or the next participant in line gets testy.

****

Since writing the above, I installed an AC/DC event between two tall southern pines that were no more than 17 feet apart.

For the pulley support a 3" OD pipe was hauled into position about 10'

above the level of the two platforms (which were installed level to one another). The two ROSA Super Pulleys (sealed roller bearings) were attached to the pipe via two drilled-through 1/2" drop forged nut eye bolts. These two nut eye bolts were located approximately 6' away (respectively) from the two support trees. The pulleys were attached to the nut eye bolts with a 1/2" rapid link. The eyes of the bolts are oriented parallel to the pipe so that the pulley sheaves

are also oriented parallel to one another and in line with the pipe. This positioning is necessary so that the KM 111 rope runs fairly through the two pulley sheaves.

The pipe was attached to one support tree with two drilled-through 1/2" X 8" lag screws. The other end was supported by a generously sized tree limb with approx. 6' of pipe projecting beyond the limb. This allowed the trees to sway independently and not exert pressure on the pipe or trees.

A section of 3/8" cable was reeved through the pipe to act as a back up to the pipe. At each end of that cable length an eye was fashioned with cable clamps or swages. Each eye was secured to the respective support trees with a well driven 1/2" staple.

At each end of the pipe a 10' long section of double eye-swaged cable was located as a back up for the pulleys. One end of the cable was well stapled into the support tree approx. 6' above the pipe and the other eye-swaged end (with 1/2 rapid link attached) was positioned (using gaffer tape on the pipe) below a pulley so that the KM 111 rope would feed freely through the link.

The ends of the KM 111 rope were tied together so that a continuous loop was formed, precluding possible loss of the rope through the pulleys. With the continuous loop extant, tag lines were not necessary. If the participant weight ratio is excessive (over 50-60 lbs. BEWARE).

A heavy participant on the ground can be assisted up by pulling on the tree-based participant's down-rope. If a participant in the UP position is heavy, their descent can be controlled by "belaying" the ascending participant's rope.

A White Elephant and A Winner

As you explain the challenge and rules of the low ropes course element-*The Wild Woosey* to your group, offer them the use of a 2" X 20" length of PVC pipe, to be used as best fits their imagination. Emphasize that the pipe cannot make contact with the ground.

If they try to use the pipe as a counterforce object; i.e., leaning back against one another while holding onto opposite ends of the pipe, they will soon discover the meaning of "white elephant."

If the performing pair decides to use the pipe as a means of establishing a firm and comfortable grip between one another, applaud that decision afterward as, "useful and safe thinking." Use of the dowel in this way precludes the unsafe practice of intertwining fingers, and also allows a greater sense of control between partners.

Paint the dowel a bright color to make it appear to be something it isn't, and to add to the festive aire of funambulistic adventure. Funambulism *is* a word, not a Rohnkeism — better look it up.

Design part of your debrief to cover "attractiveness of the quick fix", mentioning how easy it is to be seduced by theoretical solutions, rather than learning from trial & error attempts and the positive mental attitude of *failing forward*.

Harder For Hire

I don't necessarily try to make things harder, it just seems to happen.

If you have set up a 4" X 6" solidly anchored beam walk in the rafters of a gym or between two support trees, you know that walking across it (on belay, of course) will be a substantial initial challenge for students. And for most students, dealing with a 5 1/2" walking surface many feet above the ground is enough. BUT, if you're looking for more challenge, here 'tis.

Obviously, if you give the 4X6 board a quarter turn, the walking surface is reduced to 3 1/2", but that's not the unique challenge that Dave Klim and I conceptualized recently. Check this out. If the walking board is set on edge so that 3 1/2" is available for walking/balancing, up the ante by screwing/gluing on shorter sections of 4X4 boards to produce a pyramid, step-like traverse. (See photo) For example, if your walking board is 16 feet long, cut a 12' section of 4X4 and lag it to the walking surface of the 4X6. Then cut another length of 4X4, this time 8' long, and nail it to the top of the 16' 4X4. Cut a 6' length of 4X4 and ... Get it? While walking across the board you are also walking up, then down a series of pyramid-like steps.

Don't forget that walking up these steps is putting you closer to the overhead belay cable. Just make sure that the cable is high enough to preclude someone grabbing for it.

The Jeebie Lunge

The high ropes course event called *The Heebie Jeebie* has never been one of my favorite events. Admittedly it's up in the air, looks daunting and can cause a quickening of the pulse, but once you see someone else accomplish the cross-

ing (operating either above or below the foot cable) it's no big deal. It is also a high event that can result in a genuine rescue scenario; a rope-wrapped and trapped student as compared to a get-me-down-from-here lament. Obviously

just my personal opinion — I know some folks who think the H/J is the greatest.

Builders in Australia are currently putting up something called a *Jeebie*, essentially half a Heebie Jeebie. The participating student starts off with the descending rope in hand (just like the H/J), but the *Heebie* rope is missing. From a severely bent over position, the student must then try to scoot along the remaining blank section of cable to the far support tree. This is not an event completed by many participants, unless the belayer is very generous with a tensioned rope. But it gave me an idea that makes the Jeebie more functional as a completeable high event, and actually increases the challenge... or prolongs it.

Hang a section of 3/4" multiline rope from the belay cable, eight feet away from the support tree. The end of the rope should hang about three feet above the foot cable. The angled Jeebie rope should meet the foot cable about 3 feet from where the hanging rope would bisect the foot cable. (That's unavoidably wordy — check out the illustration).

When a vertical participant reaches the end of their Jeebie rope, they commit to a lunge for the rope, kind of like the Multi-Vine rope-to-rope move except from a less stable bent over position.

Note that the belay pulley will be stopped by the dangling 3/4" rope hanging 8 feet away from the support tree. This should not be a problem if the belayer situates themselves properly to prevent a pendulum fall with resultant zip. If a fall occurs right next to the tree (unlikely since the participant will have the rope in their hand) pendulum action away from the tree is unavoidable, but a well situated belayer can prevent a belay pulley from zipping back down the belay cable. In any case, the dangling student can be quickly lowered to the ground.

Magnum Limb Removal

I had the good fortune to facilitate a workshop in Tasmania at a facility about half way between the towns of Hobart and Launceston called Fawlty Towers. The John Cleese sit-com connection with Fawlty Towers is accurate as explained by our hosts Scott and Jan Marshall, the entrepreneurial owners and operators of this interesting venue.

Scott literally built his outdoor education/camping facility in the middle of an empty paddock by moving in prefab buildings and planting a plethora of trees and shrubs. During this development time, many seemingly unsurmountable obstacles were overcome, and along the way Scott compared his on-going hassles with those fabricated situations appearing then weekly on the British TV sit-com, Fawlty Towers; the name stuck and was formalized as the operating camp's corporate name.

While there, Scott invited me out to take a look at his high ropes course, a well constructed course that he had built himself with considerable phone support from Project Adventure Australia (just north in Victoria).

As I slid into the front seat of his "ute" (pronounced *yoot*; for utility vehicle) I had to move aside two scoped rifles resting on the floor boards. They were obviously well used "tools", displaying a dusty/worn appearance. Scott made no mention of the rifles, so I asked if he had been doing some hunt-

ing, thinking that perhaps he had been varminting (Tasmanian Devils were abundant in the area as evidenced by the numerous road kills; a ferocious little animal perhaps, but kind of stupid). He answered matter of factly, "No, the rifles were used primarily for dead limb removal on the ropes course", and he dropped the subject. I had to ask for details, and he seemed surprised that I was interested.

Blasting dead limbs off trees with a high caliber weapon is just not something that you can get away with in the ole U.S. of A., particularly not where PA has been doing a lot of building recently; urban/suburban New Jersey. But it makes sense in Tasmania, and I'm glad to be able to pass along this esoteric tidbit of ropes course maintenance. I have to admit, clearing dead limbs with a rifle seems a lot more fun and *safer* than having to climb 50-75 feet with a chainsaw in tow.

I suspect some of you reading this don't know where Tasmania is geo-graphically situated. Take a look at a world map, and notice the apparently small island just south of Melbourne in Australia. I know it seems an impossibly long distance away (It is! - 12,000+ miles), but if you are planning a vacation trip to OZ, make sure you venture on down to "Tassie", the hiking and wilderness areas are superb. And, if you are looking for a both rustic and comfortable place to stay during your travels, try Fawlty Towers, Fingal Valley, Tasmania 7214; Attn: Scott or Jan Marshall.

Webbing (Nylon Sling) Anchors

The use of commercial slings is such an obvious solution for low ropes course cable anchors that I hesitate to mention their use, but I will...

Get hold of an industrial catalog (try *Indusco*) that lists the use of cable, chains, winches, hauling equipment, etc. If you can't find such a catalog, look in the yellow pages for an industrial supplier. In a proper catalog you'll find a wide selection of pre-made hauling slings. These super slings are made for lifting objects of considerable weight, indeed heavier than the entire tree you are contemplating as a support anchor.

A commercial 2" two-ply nylon sling is rated at 11,200 lbs. An 8" two-ply sling is rated at 50,600 lbs. Got any houses to lift? If you are using 3/8" cable to walk on, the cable itself displays considerably less tensile strength than an 8" webbing connector.

Look for a pre-made sling that will encircle your chosen support anchor (tree, pole, concrete pillar), then add a few feet so that the two sewn eyes, (or triangular forged hardware, if you want to pay more) at the end of the sling can be clipped easily together with a rapid link. You don't want the connecting rapid link to end up right next to the support anchor, neither do you want it located more than a couple feet away from the anchor. If the link is too close to the support, attachment will be difficult and strength of the system will be compromised. If the link is some distance from the support, the attachment begins to look cumbersome.

The benefit of using a commercial sling precludes having to place a permanent anchor in the support (through bolt, peripheral bolting), and also allows a put up/take down capability.

If you plan to arrange a one day adventure training at a conference center that does not have a ropes course, you will probably find that the grounds people are predictably solicitous of their climax growth trees. Recommending the use of these wide diameter pre-made slings makes you sound and appear more professional during pre-conference discussions as to how you plan to set up your initiative apparatus. Buildings and grounds people do not like the words "through bolting" or "permanent connectors".

To establish a taut section of cable between sling supports, measure the distance between the extended slings, and cut a section of 5/16" cable that equals that distance minus 10". Swage a thimbled eye in each end of that cable. (Each swage will use up about 8 inches of cable.)

Attach one end of the cable (swaged eye) to one of the slings using a 1/2" rapid link. (Attach the link through both eyes of the sling.) When extended, the other swaged eye will be about 20" short of the far anchor sling. Connect that eye to the sling with an extended 5/8" H&H turnbuckle. (H&H stands for hook & hook; i.e., the hook arrangement at each end of the turnbuckle. This particular turnbuckle will extend to 24".) With someone holding the cable to keep it from spinning, tighten the turnbuckle until the cable is taut enough for the chosen event.

While tightening, use a large Vice-grip pliars to hold the cable eye to prevent the cable from turning. You, or someone, will also have to hold the end of the sling to prevent it from spinning. Use a 1/2 - 5/8" diameter hardwood rod to achieve the last couple tightening turns of the turnbuckle body; even your massive forearms (which should be well pumped by now) can't accomplish those final 360° turns.

Toe Hang

Been across the *Two Line Bridge*, aka *The Postman's Walk*? Done it blindfolded? Tried sitting on the bottom cable without using your hands? So what else can I do out here coach? Tried a toe hang? I didn't think so. Here's how.

Walk to the center of the element and with the aid of your belay rope sit on the bottom cable. Again, using the belay rope, lower yourself backwards into a knee hang, (don't do this with shorts on). From here you can let go of the rope and hang upside down just for the fun of it, but if you do make sure you have the stomach muscles to regain the cable with your hands (to continue into a toe hang) or gravity will dictate your next direction — down.

With the cable tucked inside the bend of your legs, and both hands on the

cable also, detach your legs from the cable and move them to the other side of the cable so that you can set your insteps (just above the base of your toes on both feet) onto the cable. Then using the belay rope for support, lower yourself slowly into a toe hang. Let go of the rope and let your arms dangle below your head with your hands in a finger

spread position, (looks good in the photos).

Some timid but well meaning folks in the past have called this hot dogging or showing off. I disagree. Escalating the basic challenge in a safe and sequential way allows those participants who want to continue their personal challenge to do so.

The Hour Glass or Infinity Traverse

This has got to be one of the easiest put up/take down elements on the low ropes course, and one of the hardest to accomplish. It's also easy to build, which is why I'm trying to tweak your interest.

Considering that you *are* interested, find two support trees about 25' apart and where the ground inbetween is uncluttered. Prune off any limbs that grow into that space.

Drive a 1/2" staple into one of the supports about 12" off the ground so that the curved end of the staple is pointing toward the other support tree. If the tree is a hardwood you would be better off to predrill the trunk before slamming the staple home. Place another similarly oriented staple 7' above the first staple. Use a hand sledge for placing the staples; a claw hammer is not heavy enough for the job.

Place two more 1/2" staples in the far support tree (same measurements) so

that the four staples are pointing toward one another. Use a near vertical (oblique) orientation to the trunk when banging in the staples. Perfectly vertical placement can cause splitting of the trunk and horizontal placement is not as strong.

Cut a section of 3/4" multiline rope to fit between a high staple on one tree to a low staple on the other tree, and add eight feet. Cut a duplicate length of rope to use between the other two staples.

Perform a thimbled eye splice in one end of the rope. If you don't know how to splice, tie a figure eight loop in the end of the rope instead. If you are going to do this add ten feet to the length of each rope, rather than eight: the knot uses up more rope than a splice. Do the same splice or knot arrangement in the second rope also.

Clip a non-locking carabiner into the eye splice and snap it into one of the high staples. Take the other end of that

rope and reeve it (pass it) through the low staple in the far support tree. Take the working end of the rope and tie a prusik knot onto the standing part of the rope. Utilizing the unique characteristics of the prusik knot, tighten up that length of rope. Perform the same arrangement with the second rope. Done.

The objective is to get from one support tree to another without touching the ground inbetween: i.e.,traverse the crossing ropes.

This low element is quite difficult and needs to be spotted closely (two spotters minimum) as falls are frequent and unannounced.

To increase the difficulty of the event place two more staples so that each support tree also has staples at five feet above the ground. When the ropes are shifted to the second set of staples the "Hour Glass" will be more extended and the degree of difficulty will have increased considerably.

The Not-So Wobbly Walk

The *Wobbly Walk*, a low ropes course event that was mildly popular in the early 70's, was not one of my favorite elements to build — very labor intensive. Each Wobbly Walk (a series of 2X6 planks bolted onto vertical ground supported 4X4's) needed at least six walking segments to be worth doing. Six walking planks required twelve 4X4 supports; i.e., 12 post holes. If the digging was hard (roots, rocks, fill) a Wobbly Walk could literally consume hours of back breaking *PHD labor.

Here's how to install a low Wobbly Walk without having to dig one hole or bolt any planks. If you're not interested after that dynamite intro, ropes course construction just isn't your thing.

Purchase the following:

- ❑ Eight lengths of pressure treated 2X4 boards that vary in length from 6' to 14'.
- ❑ Approx. 30 - 3/8" X 12" common nail spikes

Measure along the edge of each 2X4 board and make a mark every 18". Drill *through the width* of the board at each mark with a 7/16" drill bit. Make your best effort to drill "on the plumb" or use a drill press if available.

Determine where you want your *Not-So Wobbly Walk* to be located, put the boards down on edge, insert the spikes into the holes, and, using a hammer, drive them into the turf. If the ground isn't too hard you can "step in" the spikes.

Do not try to set up your boards on sandy soil, the spikes will not hold well enough to hold the boards steady. After you are finished with the event, and to remove the boards, pull up on one end of the board about 8", then pull up the opposite end. Remove the loosened spikes and store the boards 'till next time.

Long boards do not "spike" well on uneven ground. If the ground is uneven, use shorter boards, and more of them.

My wife, Gloree, uses the boards as part of her portable initiative obstacle course.

Pre-Crimping a Swage

How's that for an exciting bit of rubric? Just makes you want to go out and find a swage to pre-crimp, eh? If

you use swages as a cable connector for ropes course construction, the following bit of information will be useful and marginally interesting, otherwise...

*PHD = Post Hole Digger

A nico-press swage is an extruded bit of metal (the metalurgy of the swage varies as to useage), usually in the shape of an extruded oval or figure-eight cut-off tube. The cable to be connected, or made into a "swaged" eye, is reeved through the nico-press swage once and then back onto itself, so when the swage is crimped the two cable sections are squeezed tightly together forming a tight bond between swage and cable; actually more than the full tensile strength of the cable itself. (Just be-cause... I once cut a swaged cable joint in half with a hack saw, and was im-pressed that the comparatively soft metal of the swage had been squeezed *between* the strands of the cable.)

When a builder is swaging alone (a swaging tool for 5/16" cable weighs 14 unwieldy pounds) an ongoing hassle is how to keep the double reeved cable in position; i.e., from slipping, until you have had a chance to perform the first of three standard crimps.

Try this, Oh ye solo swager: Reeve the cable end through the swage and back onto itself, then adjust the working end of the cable so that it peeks just beyond the end of the swage by about 1/4" (As an aside—you need that extra 1/4" because when the swage is crimped, the malleable metal of the swage end will be squeezed beyond the cable end if the cable is flush with the end of the swage *before* the crimp.) And finally — the tip, the advice, the raison d'être for these esoteric paragraphs.

Use a vice grip to squeeze just the side of the swage through which the working end of the cable is reeved. This minimum compression will hold the cable in place until you perform the first of three full swaging compressions with the larger swaging tool.

Wow, was it worth it? Not unless you are doing multiple swages alone or swaging at the top of a ladder, then it's worth the entire price of the book! But, hey... that's life, isn't it? Some people swage, some people hedge, some people wedge. (A wedger is someone who gives wedgies).

Sledge Hammer

Recognizing that this tidbit of ropes course gear paraphanalia is somewhat esoteric, and in deference to the suspect-ed limited interest in customizing your hand sledge — I'll be brief.

I use my hand sledge frequently for driving staples, starting lag screws, and convincing other stubbon bits of steel and wood that I am as stubborn if not as tough. Sometimes (rarely ...rarely) my aim is a bit off center, and the sledge handle takes the brunt of my misdirect-ed muscle. Here's a way to protect the handle and also customize/personalize your own moljinar.

Cut a 48" length of #4 nylon cord (parachute cord). Using the same "whipping" technique that you would use to finish off the cut end of a rope, whip the cord onto the throat of the hammer handle just below the sledge head. Pull each wrap tightly and finish off with a goodly tug. You should end up with about 15 turns of cord around the handle. As is, this whipping looks pretty good and will both personalize and protect your sledge handle from occasional over zealous blows, but without further protection the cord will soon begin to unravel.

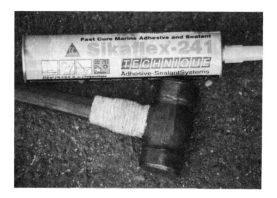

To further the aesthetics and function (prevent unraveling), coat the multiple wraps of cord with a copious layering of the marine adhesive SIKAFLEX; (comes in a caulking-type tube; black or white — see photo). This adhesive is super strong, but more significantly for this application, remains flexible when cured.

So what else are you not interested in?

Alternate Anchor Zip

All you need for the AA Zip is a 150' length of 11 mm KM 111 rope, 30' of 3/4" multiline rope; a wall installed platform (or convenient balcony arrangement); a ROSA aluminum sheave, roller bearing pulley (with carabiners and double eye spliced rope attacher); a wall or beam eye bolt anchor at the start of the ride; about ten committed people, and a bundle of balls (the gonad type).

Tie or clip one end of the KM 111 to a through-the-wall drop forged eye bolt (or some other bomb proof anchor) that has been installed about 8-9 feet above the platform standing area. Drop the loose working end of the rope to your anchor group below. Using a double fisherman's knot, tie the lengths of KM 111 and 3/4" multiline together. The larger diameter multiline allows a better gripping size and feel than the KM 111.

Install your ROSA snatch block pulley onto the rope, clip in (locking crabs) the 3' double spliced-eye rope connector between the pulley and your harness. (Yes, YOUR harness; you have a moral responsibility to try this first.)

Standing ready and alert on the platform, alert the anchor team that you are ready to zip. As soon as your intrep-

id holders have backed up to apply the requisite tension, detach yourself from the platform and zip away.

If you want a better idea of what "...requisite tension" means before you zip, do this: standing on the floor, attach your pulley to the zip rope. Ask your rope holders to to apply tension, then, holding onto the zip pulley attachment rope, run away from the holding group so that your pulley is rolling up the rope. If the group is applying "requisite tension" you should have no trouble zipping a few feet off the floor and the holders should have no trouble supporting your weight.

As you glide toward the *wood* floor of the gym, adjust your feet parallel to the parquet and finish off your ride with a satisfying slide-to-a-stop. Provide large tube-type socks to pull over the rider's shoes to facilitate the floor slide. If the gym surface is rubberized (no sliding surface), *do not use this event*, as someone will eventually land with locked knees...

Coming in backward is not allowed, but happens regularly, so you might as well say it's okay. Just suggest that the rider drag their feet when it seems appropriate.

If the tie-in bolt height is above 25', ream out a cable zip brake block hole so that a section of 1/2" KM 111 can be reeved through that routed hole. Cut the block in half (it's already cut in half

linearly), and screw in two type O eye screws, one on each side. Attach a 25' length of 1/2" bungee to each eye screw, (see photo). Reeve the bungee through the eye screw hole and tie a figure eight knot into the end of the bungee.

If the starting height is above 30', lower it.

Swinging Trapeze

Sure, I know, all trapezes swing, but I'm talking about using a trapeze instead of a swing rope for low initiative problems. For example, on the Nitro Crossing or Disc Jockeys.

Don't dismiss this idea or just read-on-by. Here's why... In the past I have always spliced a loop into the bottom of most swing ropes so that folks who are *well covered* or don't have the upper

body strength to support their body weight can put their foot into the loop before swinging. This works okay, but it requires boosting the participant up so that they can fit their foot into the loop, then requires a later group effort to get their foot out at the destination end of the swing's pendulum.

If you hang a trapeze from the bottom of a swing cable/rope the swinger gets a better initial, two handed, parallel grip. If the feeling is that more support is needed, all the swinger has to do is tuck the trapeze under their arm pits (no boosting required), pick up their feet and swing away. Upon arrival at the far end of the pendulum arc, detaching from the trapeze is as simple as raising your arms.

A Pamper Pole-type trapeze works fine. Attach two short sections of rope (knotted or eye spliced) to each trapeze eye bolt, then use a carabiner to clip the two ends of the ropes together. Clip that carabiner into the end of the swing rope. Use it!

The trapeze should measure no more than 4 feet to the ground at the bottom of the pendulum arc.

The Vertical Trapeze

If you don't orient carabiners and rapid links in the gate-down position (so that the screw gate rotates toward the center of the earth), a rare few will unscrew themselves (open) over time due to gravity and jostling around. This is a ropes course truism which unfortunately has been experienced and verified over and over.

Sometimes, due to the above mentioned bouncing around, the rapid link reorients itself into the gate-up position and unscrews itself without your help. To prevent this, tighten the gates with an adjustable wrench — now wait a minute — not THAT much! You might want to remove this connector someday. In fact, if you plan to leave the rapid link out there for the entire season, or maybe even a year or so, you better deliver a dolop of grease to the threads, otherwise a hack saw replaces the wrench.

I hadn't planned for this to be a lesson in ropes course maintenance, but it's good stuff to know. The reason I mentioned the unscrewed rapid link in the first place, was because of something that happen recently on the Project Adventure Pamper Pole trapeze.

Because of a gravity loosened rapid link, one half of the trapeze support cable detached from the overhead suspension cable. This happened while a ready-to-jump participant was balancing on top of the pole. (The belay cable and trapeze had just been jostled by another person jumping from an adjacent Pamper Plank for a trapeze that is connected to the same cable.) If you didn't understand that last parenthetical reference, don't bother re-reading it, just picture someone standing on top of the Pamper Pole, struggling desperately for balance and sputtering that half his target had just disengaged, which indeed it had. The vertically dangling trapeze apparently did not present an attractive challenge to that not-so-stable person, so he decided to climb down — Challenge by Joyce; that was his belayer's name. But it looked challenging to me, so I tied in (good ole bowline around the waist, keeps you honest) and had a dive at the raggedly surreal vertical section of PVC rod. I caught it fairly, did a couple pull-ups, and was subsequently lowered down.

Reflecting on that visually bizarre challenge, I decided to replace what was there (definitely untidy) with a *store-bought* vertical trapeze. We already had another conventional horizontal trapeze for the Pamper Plank dive, so this new vertical challenge was well received.

The vertical trapeze has been in use for at least five years, and from my observations, about 80% grab the bar.

firmly, and of those, perhaps one in three will hold on. I'm not sure if it's because they grab, then relax, or maybe just a relationship of body weight to arm strength, but the results are predictable — rapid descent and a strong desire to try it again.

To build this unique vertical target, take a 3-foot section of inch and a quarter diameter PVC rod or any kind of similar diameter hardwood dowel, and drill a 3/8" hole one and a half inch in from the end. Then, either eye swage a section of 1/4" cable or eye splice a length of 1/2" multiline rope through that hole. The length of the cable or rope should be such as to hang the center of the trapeze at about chest level to the jumper. Rough up the bar with a rasp to provide the best grip. A smooth section of PVC rod is a bad joke. You might even want to provide a rosin bag for the jumpers, as sweaty palms are a common by-product of this event.

This is a useful variation to the normal trapeze jump, (you gotta be kidding, none of this stuff is normal). A tip from an experienced jumper and observer — when you go for it, grab high on the bar, squeeze like the devil, and *keep your arms bent.* If you grab at the bottom of the bar with straight arms, the immediate drop is impressive.

Opinions/Tips

Always, always...

Even if you have a large group, at some point during the first couple hours of a session, always play *Toss-A-Name Game* (**Bottomless Bag Again !?**, pg. 8). I have on occasion left out this active and useful name game and have always been sorry that I did. How's come?

❑ People react with more compassion and friendliness to other people in the group if they have a *handle* to use other than, "Hey you!"
❑ A feeling of "groupness" invariably results after spending the 20 minutes or so involved in this game.

❑ Social barriers are drooped (that's correct, *drooped*, not *dropped*) and people become more socially receptive as the result of taking a chance (in this case playing a game that is unfamiliar) and then finding out that things are still OK.

If your group is too large (over 25) to play the game efficiently, find a way (helpers) to split the group for the initial name learning.

Monday Morning Ruminations

Caveat - I'm adding right now to what I think is one of the increasing communication problems that we all face, the proliferation of the printed word, but I don't know how else to lay this huge truism on you — *All this adventure curriculum stuff is simple; the material, the presentation, the pre and post conversations: simple.*

Don't try to make it hard. If you can't present what you know in such a way that the students like it, benefit from the results, and want more, find another curriculum approach, otherwise all this good stuff will evolve faster'n a fruit fly into the 3 R's, fizz ed approach; "Rollin' out the ropes, readin' the roll, and reee-laxin'."

Group Size

I can't say with certainty at what size a group becomes too large to ensure an optimum experience, but part of the variable has to do with how long you will be working with the group. I can comfortably present games and initiatives in a conference setting to over 50 people, if I know that the experience will be limited to a couple hours. If I'm going to be with the group for the day, twenty participants would be more workable. If the training is a multiple day scenario, then 15-18 participants would be ideal. These are numbers that I am comfortable with, but obviously someone less experienced with facilitating or working with a less motivated group, might feel more effective with smaller numbers at the high end.

Recently I was working with a group of 33 teachers for a full day games and initiative workshop. The games were well received and even though I had to project my voice, at the end of the day I still had some voice left. On the following day the number of participants for the same type of training clinic increased to 42, and my presentation problems increased considerably; i.e., well beyond the problems that 11 more people should have represented. During that morning session people felt left out and unattended. There was also a feeling of impersonality and not getting a chance to really experience the activities as much as they would have liked. I felt frustrated by not being able to communicate with everyone, feeling as if I were talking to only part of the group, and speaking much louder than I would have liked. Also because of the large group size I didn't get a chance to cover as much material as I could have with half that number of people.

Fortunately, during the afternoon session I had two assistants to help. Splitting the group into three smaller groups made all the difference. People responded better to the activities, laughed more, and left the workshop satisfied that they had gotten what they came for. Don't stuff your workshops in order to pay bills; the quality of the experience suffers.

Negative Comments and Timing

I can't think of a circumstance when negative comments made during your introductory presentation serve any purpose, even if they are offered in a positive way.

Talking with a workshop group to which I had just been introduced, I unthinkingly began talking about safety factors on the ropes course. My purpose was to allay any fears they might have about height, rope strength, falling, etc., but the things I found myself saying was achieving just the opposite. I wasn't saying anything that wouldn't have been well accepted by the same group on the third or forth day of the clinic: good intentions - bad timing.

Play

Criteria for pure play: spontaneous, no recorded scores, no winner/loser scenarios, laughter, joy...

Play can obviously be experienced by one person, but the fun aspect is enhanced by sharing the situation with other players. I've developed an ability over the years to include people in play situations that they would have had difficulty initiating themselves.

As the result of growing up as an only child and being part of a military service family, I often found myself in situations where I had to entertain (play by) myself. I became efficient at this level of self play, and can remember situations where I avoided other children who I knew were not as play oriented; i.e., more into the adolescent social scene of dances, parties and hanging out with their peers.

When I was asked to help develop an innovative physical education curriculum, as part of the initial 1971 Project Adventure grant, I didn't think much about the challenge or ramifications of the responsibility, because I responded to it as just that, an occupational responsibility. As we got into the day-to-day curriculum requirements of coming up with something unique to fill the class time, I did what had always come easy, playing with the students, or more specifically letting them play with me. The activities that were being lauded as so innovative and educationally sound were reconstructed of scenarios from 30 to 40 years earlier: shadows of my childhood were being replayed.

I'd like to say that there was a lot of thought and planning put into the initial activities that eventually made it into

PA's first curriculum book, *Cowstails &
Cobras,* but almost invariably the play
and innovation were the result of neces-
sity (What are we going to do today?)
and my subsequent playful reaction to
the situation, the people, the weather,
what I had or didn't have for breakfast...

This is not to say that each morning I
came up with sparkling new activities
that turned everyone on to physical
education and life, but as different
situations presented themselves (a new
semester, different schools, a curriculum
requirement, unique environments) the
opportunity for trying something new
often dovetailed with a pleasant or
exciting play-memory from the past that
I could change or embellish to fulfill the
day's need.

As I became more aware of what was
required on a daily basis, I began to
think and day dream about what was
relatively safe, physically possible and
fun. The combination of people depend-
ing upon me for innovative ideas, a
natural creative proclivity, and some
undeniable ego fulfillment, continued
my initial flow of ideas, ploys and plans.
It must be habit forming, I'm still doing
it.

Rapport

❑ Develop a sense of rapport with the
students right from the git go.
❑ Don't give the group a chance to not
like you.

❑ Don't start lecturing or begin speaking as if you are the instructor.
❑ Think about *casual competence.* Try to
be casual in your presentation,

- ❑ Begin your sessions conversationally.
- ❑ Tell them something that happened to you recently of consuming interest; it doesn't even have to relate to the workshop or what you plan to teach.
- ❑ Sit with or among the students during your sessions. Be Socratic.

Teaching vs. Facilitating vs. Teaching

Just back from a Project Adventure workshop and loaded with new curriculum "stuff", you will, like any conscientious teacher, plan for many more activities than you could possibly fit into a 4, 6 or 8 hour inservice training day. Your first instructional day will probably end with a "bag full" of unused activities, or you may fall prey to the if-you-got-it-you-better-use-it quick-draw syndrome which characterizes itself with a display of machine gun-like presentations of your prepared material.

The cause is insidious and difficult to resist. As the day progresses you recognize that the participants are having an increasingly good time and that this high level of enjoyment apparently depends entirely upon the unique characteristics of the activities themselves. The anxious feeling develops that you better keep feeding the fires-of-fun or they will soon discover that, "the king is not wearing any clothes"; i.e., you're as conceptually naked as a 3rd grade book report. Now obviously that's not true, because you *are* a certified teacher and have had *beau coup* hours of hands-on experience with other learners just like the ones in front of you, ecstatically anticipating the next activity. BUT, "What *are* we going to do next?"

Don't fret about my penchant for Pollyannic predictions, or more annoyingly, for having "hit the nail on the pedagogic head." Rapid fire presentation of prepared material is not uncommon at first, resulting from your enjoyment of the unique activities (no push ups here, good buddy) and the enthusiastic response of the students. This is heady stuff, and the temptation is to keep student enthusiasm at a peak.

There's nothing wrong with occasionally wallowing in some well deserved fun and positive feed back, but also recognize that an approach that's pure Sesame Street (impossibly entertaining education) is bound to wind down eventually. Which is not to say that there isn't enough curriculum fuel to operate at a high level of enjoyment for a considerable time, but reflect on what you are missing if you toss out one activity after another just because, "...the kids are obviously having a good time."

Another consideration: your students are experiencing more than just the physical joy of participating. Some might harbor consistent (daily) fears about all this curriculum excitement, others might like more time to conceptually digest what is occurring within the group, and a few might need the opportunity just to express what they are emotionally experiencing as the result of interfacing with the group. My point is, you HAVE TO offer the group an occasional activity break in order to process the developing interrelationships, fears, joys, uncertainty, conceptual break-throughs, and all the myriad cognitive/affective experiences that will psychologically boil over or be tragically ignored if time is not set aside for some simple honest conversation. I don't want to seem too demanding about this, but you **HAVE TO**, otherwise all that you're presenting is an effective recreation program, and Project Adventure activities offer the opportunity for much more than that.

Don't get in a dither about having to "facilitate a pseudo-psychiatric session", that's not what you should be attempting to accomplish anyway. I agree, most teachers do not have the psychological or psychiatric training to facilitate an in-depth character and personality debriefing; that's not what you have been trained to accomplish. Just try to set up a *comfortable conversational situation* among the people who have just experienced something significant together. The purpose for processing (debriefing, reviewing) a jointly shared experience is to allow the participants to individually express themselves in a supportive, trusting, non-judgemental atmosphere — PERIOD.

Try not to let the stimulating and revealing, but largely superficial dia-

logue tempt you to role-play Freud and get yourself into deep psychiatric doo doo. As trust is slowly established between newly met people, and as those individuals participate together, playing games and trying to solve initiative problems, there should be a planned continuation of that trust to include normal handling of emotions toward one another during potentially risky people-to-people contact. One of your program goals *must* be to establish a level of physical and emotional trust among participants. Without trust there will be little or no progress made toward achieving any other individual or program goals.

I read myself above as uncharacteristically directive, particularly my italicized *suggestions,* but I want you to know how strongly I feel about their implementation. Using PA techniques does not require a keen intellect or extensive training, but all this proven good stuff *can* be screwed up by an unthinking or inappropriate use of the philosophy and teaching tools; I've seen it happen.

An unfortunate and encompassing problem is that many young people in this country have been taught as a societal norm, not to trust, and from a win/lose competitive standpoint, to recognize and exploit any perceived weakness in others toward attaining their own goal — to win. Team work, other than in competitive sports, is not emphasized other than the expected lip service paid to pie-in-the-sky curriculum models. And when team work *is* emphasized (little league sports) the team becomes the individual as above, trying to exploit the weakness of the other team, etc. etc.

Trust needs to be consistently empha-sized, nurtured, and protected. Tell the group flat-out that you want them — need them — to trust one another. Give positive feedback when someone goes out of their way to help an "opponent" from getting hurt or devalued. If I'm bigger than you, and it's obvious that we are both going to arrive at the ball simultaneously, it becomes my responsi-bility NOT to use my size to hip-check you away from the ball to gain an advantage. It is further my responsibility (and yours) to care enough that we fend off each other rather than making prede-termined, purposeful and predictably one-sided contact.

I have chastised many adults in workshops (and did not enjoy the *responsible* role) for disregarding a trusting atmosphere in order to achieve a cheap laugh. (tickling a blindfolded person, letting that sightless person wander into jeopardy, tasteless jokes about body size, etc.) There is no doubt in my mind that you can have hilarious belly-splitting fun during games without taking advantage of another's person's weakness or vulnerable position.

When you first get together with a group as their facilitator, take your time. You don't have to WOW them immedi-ately. Start an interesting conversation as people begin to collect. Ask them if anyone knows what the world's fastest animal is? After you have heard the predictable answers ...cheetah, African bot flies, or hawks in a stoop, tell them, *it's a cow that has been pushed out of a*

helicopter. Before they stop laughing, or before they wonder why you asked, ask them if they have seen the movie *Point Break*. Then rhapsodize about the "way cool" sky diving scenes and how many miles per hour a falling body (a cow?) can achieve. Capture their interest. Do some reading about what they might be interested in. Take in a movie that they might see and talk about. Talk about dugongs, recent volcanic activity, new electronic gimmicks, pain inflicted by the insidious Candiru fish...

Now, indicate that you have a few fun things to do that they might like to try. Emphasize the *Challenge By Choice* credo, but also emphasize the difference between occasionally not trying and being consistently unwilling to try. Then hit 'em with a GOOD game. Don't take any chances here, use an activity that you have had luck with in the past. There will be lots of time in the future with this group when they can unrea-sonably respond to your trial and error, guinea-pig-game attempts, (Karl... you gotta be kidding—this game sucks!) but now is not the time.

MOON BALL is a consistent winner for me. Not many rules to offer, people can play or not play without seeming studly or whimpish, and the level of involvement is infectiously high. Check out the rules in one of those game books that PA sells.

Finally, (I always breathe a little easier when some one says, "finally..." because I know my commitment to listening or reading is coming to an end. Not that I don't necessarily like what is being communicated, I just like to be in control of my ambient sensory input), *resist the temptation to do what you have been trained to do : teach.*

You are there as a facilitator to establish a comfortable, working/playing situation, frame (brief) the instructional tool being used, set & enforce safety parameters, keenly observe behaviors and group interaction, and be available afterwards to *facilitate* discussion and learning. If you resort to teaching; i.e., offering instructional tips or hints to facilitate a solution, you are reducing the experiential value for the group and the satisfaction that comes from solving a problem *by themselves*. Your ego must take a back seat to the group's ego. The applause that spontaneously occurs when a group is happy with their performance is not for you, they are cheering themselves. You can smile and applaud too at that point, because you are doing a good job.

ADVENTURE MISCELLANY

Acronyms & Initialisms

Here's a list of interesting acronyms and initialisms. Want to know what to do with them? Print 'em up on 3X5 cards, one per card. Hand out the cards to a group and ask them to come up with as many correct answers in 15 minutes as possible. Be liberal with what's considered correct. This exercise represents a dandy method to introduce brainstorming techniques.

People are drawn to acronyms because they represent "words" used on a daily basis; RADAR and SCUBA for example. Most people know what a LASER represents, but didn't know that the letters of the acronym stand for **L**ight **A**mplification **S**erialized **E**mission **R**adiation. People are fascinated by what they don't know about what they think they should know.

How many times have you seen the acronym **NASDAQ** in the financial section of the newspaper, or **CAR-RT** stamped on sections of your daily mail delivery, or **M&M** on those tasty chocolate morsels that do melt in your hand?

Probably hundreds of times, but now you don't have to continue wondering 'cause they are all included in the list.

You say, "Who cares?" Me, I suppose. Hope you enjoy the list. Bring out this list at a get together and I think you will be surprised at the level of interest that develops. It's alphabetized only because this machine does that kind of thing.

AAHPERD - American Alliance for Health, PE, Recreation & Dance

ABCD - Above and Beyond the Call of Duty

ACLU - American Civil Liberties Union

ACRONYM - A Contrived Reduction of Nomenclature Yielding Mnemonics

AFL-CIO - American Federation of Labor & Congress of Industrial Organ.

AFSCME - American Federation of State, County, & Municipal Employees

ANSI - American National Standards Institute

ARVN - Army of the Republic of Viet Nam

AWACS - Airborne Warning & Control System

BASIC - Beginner's All-Purpose Symbolic Instruction Code (Computers)

BIONICS - Biology & Electronics

BOMFOG - Brotherhood of Man, Fatherhood of God

BOQ - Bachelor Officer's Quarters

BMX - Bicycle Motocross

CAR-RT - Carrier Route

CD-ROM - Compact Disc - Read Only Memory

CETI - Communication with Extraterrestrial Intelligence

CNN - Cable News Network

COMSAT - Communications Satellite

CPU - Central Processing Unit

D&C - Dilation & Curetage

D & D - Drunk & Disorderly

DDT - Dichlorodiphenyltrichloroethane

DNF - Did Not Finish

DOHC - Double Over-Head Cam

DOIT - Do One Important Thing (*Offered by Adrian Kissler*)

DPT - Diptheria, Pertussis, Tetanus

DUT - Dangerously Undertrained (*Coined by Project Adventure, Inc.*)

EPA - Environmental Protection Agency

ERIC - Educational Resources Information Center

ESPN - Entertainment & Sports Programming Network

EVA - Extra-Vehicular Activity

FEAR - False Evidence Appears Real (Forget Everything and Run)

FEMALE - Formerly Employed Mothers At Loose Ends

FIAT - Fabricana Italiana Automobile Torino

FILO - First In Last Out

4-H - Head, Heart, Hands, & Health

GAR - Grand Army of the Republic

GIGO - Garbage In, Garbage Out

GMT - Greenwich Mean Time

GOP - Grand Old Party

GPA - Grade Point Average

GRAS - Generally Regarded As Safe

HDL - High-Density Lipoprotein (Cholesterol)

HMO - Health Maintenance Organization

IAAF - International Amateur Athletic Federation

IOOF - Independent Order of Odd Fellows

ISSN - International Standard Serial Number

LABIA - Lesbians and Bisexuals in Alliance

LIFO - Last In, First Out

MAD - Mutual Assured Destruction

MAFIA - *Morte Alla Francia Italia Aneia* (Death to the French is Italy's Cry)

M.G. - Morris Garage

MAYDAY - *m'aidez*

M&M's - first letters of the last names of Forrest **M**ars and Bruce **M**urrie

MODEM - Modulator Demodulator

MOPED - Motorized Pedal Cycle

NASDAQ - Nat'l Assoc. of Securities Dealers Automated Quotations

NSA - National Security Agency (Never Say Anything)

NEAT - No Exercise All Talk (*Project Adventure meeting lingo*)

NECCO - New England Confectionary Co.

NICE - No Intelligent Conversation Emitted (*Offered by Dave Altman*)

NBA - Nothing But Air

NORAD - North American Aerospace Defense Command

NOW Account - Negotiable Order of Withdrawl Account

OBE - Out-of-Body Experience

OCR - Optical Character Recognition (*Oscar Carl Rohnke, my dad*)

OXFAM - Oxford Committee for Famine Relief

PAT - Point After Touchdown

P.F. Flyers - Posture Foundation

POETS - Phooey on Everything — Tomorrow's Saturday

P&Q's - Pints & Quarts (old bartender's method of keeping a tab)

PSA - Prostate Specific Antigen

PSAT - Preliminary Scholastic Appitude Test

PSWAG - Pseudo Scientific Wild Ass Guess (*offered by Adrian Kissler*)

QUANTAS - Queensland and Northern Territory Air Service

q.t. - Quiet (as, ...on the q.t.)

RADAR - Radio Detecting and Ranging

RIF - Reduction In Force

ROMEO - Retired Old Men Eating Out (*offered by Plynn Williams*)

RTFM - Read The F_____ Manual; as in, "When all else fails... RTFM!"

SAHAND - Society Against Have A Nice Day

SALT - Strategic Arms Limitation Talks

SAM - Surface to Air Missle

SCUBA - Self Contained Underwater Breathing Apparatus

S&D, S&L, S&M - Song & Dance, Savings & Loan, Sadism & Masochism

SETI - Search for Extraterrestrial Intelligence

SHAME - Society to Humilitate, Aggravate, Mortify, and Embarrass Smokers

SID - Sudden Infant Death Syndrome

SNAG - Sensitive New Age Guy

SPAM - Spiced Ham

STP - Scientifically Treated Petroleum

S.V.P. - Please (s'il vous plat)

TARMAC - Tar/Macadam (Hot Top, Bitumen, Asphalt)

TEGWAR - That Exciting Game Without Any Rules (*Heard from Gary Moore*)

TELEX - Teletype Exchange

T.I.D. - *ter in die* (three times a day)

TIPS - To Improve Personal Service

TMJ - Tempromandibular Joint

TNT - Trinitrotoluene

TWIMC - To Whom It May Concern

UNESCO - United Nations Educational, Scientific, and Cultural Organization

UNICEF - United Nations Children's Fund

USO - United Service Organization

VCR - Videocassette Recorder

VFR - Visual Flight Rules

VISTA - Volunteers in Service to America

V.S.O.P. - Very Superior Old Pale

WATS - Wide-Area Telecommunications Service

WCTU - Woman's Christian Temperance Union

WILCO - Will Comply

WISC - Wechsler's Intelligence Scale for Children

WPA - Works Progress Administration

WYSIWYG - What You See Is What You Get

YAVIS - Young, Attractive, Verbal, Intelligent, and Successful

YUMPLE - Young Upwardly Mobile Professional

YUPPIE - Young Urban Professional

YURT - You're Ultimately Responsible Together

ZIP - Zone Improvement Program

ZPG - Zero Population Growth

ZZZZ - Onomatopoeic Snoozing

I still don't know what the ubiquitous **B.U.M.** on sweatshirts stands for. Any ideas?

Mouth Manipulators

I don't like long tongue twisters, in fact I'm not fond of the genre at all. But these three are short enough to remember and tricky enough to make you and your buddies stumble over that slippery muscle in your mouth. The procedure/challenge is to mouth the two words rapidly three times, then get the fourth attempt out correctly.

❑ preshrunk shirts
❑ toy boat

❑ truly rural (If you are ever around my son Drew, have him try this one for you.)

Here's a bonus mouth full that was passed along by my good friend, John Herbert. *"I'm not a fig plucker, nor a fig plucker's son, but I can pluck figs when the fig plucker comes."* Good luck and behave yourself.

Eggs & Stuff

This doesn't have much to do with adventure education, but.... My Dad recently passed along this eggselent idea. Considering that I have known

him for the last 58 years, kind of makes you wonder how I missed out on this neat-o trick for over half a century.

I don't eat many eggs anymore because of the cholesterol thing, but I do hard-boil up a batch occasionally. I eat only the solidified albumen and throw the yolk away, or put it in the backyard bird feeder — seems appropriate somehow. Sometimes the eggs peel easily, sometimes not, but there is something that you can do to insure an easy peel every time. Simply stick a needle through the egg shell before you immerse it in boiling water. That's it, that's all... works every time. Thanks Pop.

While we're talking about eggs, you *do* know how to tell a hard boiled egg from a raw egg, right? Try to spin the egg on a hard smooth surface. If the egg spins, it's hard boiled. If the egg just falls over, (eggcentrically) it's raw. I love simple, practical stuff like this.

Have you ever thrown a raw egg at something? (That's some*thing*, not some*one*) I think you should, just to check it off your life-list of things that need to be done.

Continuing with this eggciting oviparous topic, playing catch with a raw egg

is a halfway entertaining, outdoor, summertime fun thing to do, and fulfills your *...have you ever* requirement. The idea is to begin the toss/catch — catch/toss close to one another, and, after making a successful catch/catch, gradually move farther apart until the sequence finalizes with a catch/smooch or splot/catch — thus the reference to *halfway entertaining* above. Seventy-five feet is about the best I have accomplished with a friend. Remember, this activity should be approached as a win/win, otherwise a splotch/splooch ensues.

The next time you try *Group Juggling*, substitute an egg for one of the balls. To continue that feeling of developing trust, it's probably a good idea to let the group know about the impending egg. (See Group Juggle Variations)

Which reminds me — Did you know that there is a Guiness world record for tossing and orally catching a grape between two people? Well, there is! One person throws, the other person makes their oral cavity available as a target as far downfield as possible. I remember the record as being well over 200', which is as it should be — *real* world records are all ridiculously outta sight.

If you want to be *really* humbled sometime, heft a 16 pound shot put and ask some one to stand eighty feet away as a target. (Eighty + feet is the real world for this event.) Now try to put the shot *half* that distance. No? Try 30 feet. Still no go? Try 20. Unbelieveable! So try a grape. Most anyone can throw a grape 80 feet ...and don't forget to have an orally oriented friend downfield to receive. Caveat — Don't play this game with a shot put.

Steve Butler (my partner in various serindidipidous scenarios involving radically conspicuous involvement) and I have thrown many things at one another over the years (frisbees, aerobies, comet balls, etc.), so recently decided to try to establish the somehow overlooked, Wenham, Massachusetts grape-to-mouth distance throw record.

The grapes, carefully chosen for this record attempt, were the large purplish thick skinned type with pits; i.e, the kind no one really likes, but mouths a few at a party just to be polite, then wonders what to do with the pits?

To establish our respective roles for this record attempt, we measured oral capacities and came up with about the same side-to-side (smile) diameter, but Steve had the edge from tooth to tooth, which was okay because my throwing arm is a bit stronger.

We warmed up a bit at 20-30 feet and had no problems making consistent oral contact. We did find, however, that if the grape hit Steve's teeth it sheared in half with less than a full grape ending up in situ/in toto, so to speak. There was no one present that could clarify the rules concerning this, but not wanting to establish only half a record, we conscientiously counted only those grapes that ended up wholly pocketed; i.e., a grape that was as intact a priori the throw as it was now wetly in hand.

Our best throw/catch was just over 100 feet, certainly not a world class effort, but enough to qualify as Wenham's best, and satisfying nonetheless.

Give the event a try, it's less damaging than boxing, and more fun than Eskimo cheek wrestling. Let me know if you beat 100 feet, so that I can alert Steve to make his oral cavity available again for some long distance fruit abuse.

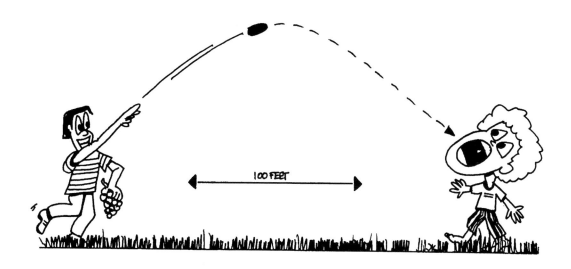

100 FEET

GAK

GAK, made available by Nickelodean Co., is available in most toy stores. A small star-shaped container (4 ozs.) costs about $3.00. Get some.

Pry up the cap and get aquainted with this oozy-goozy substance. It feels simultaneously cool and wet to the touch, and you're sure that when you put it down some of the miasmic (your-asmic) substance will remain on your hands, or at least some lingering odor will persist. Nope, Gak remains pretty much unto its tactile self, striking fear only into the hearts of expensive rug owners.

I'll bet this stuff would gross people out if used as a ball for a game. Right! Take out your Gak (Gak has to live in an air tight container between play periods or it will dessicate all over you) and roll it into a ball — I'll bet you're smiling. Use Gak to establish the people-to-people pattern used in the initiative game, *Warp Speed*.

Don't worry if your Gak is dropped and picks up dirt and grass, which it definitely has an affinity for. Now your Gak has texture, what a deal! Continue playing until Gak and dirt are indistinguishable, then spring for a new container — Hey, it's only three bucks. Dispose of Gak as you would a dead gold fish or canary. Caveat — Gak does not flush well!

The following formula for ersatz GAK was generously provided by Shirley Sutton of Canton Center, CT. She also included some of her final product *in the same envelope!* I have to admit, this stuff is very GAK-like, but the aroma of Elmer's Glue is unmistakeable. Let's call it KAG!

- ❑ 1 rounded teaspoon of 20 Mule Team Borax powder
- ❑ 8 ounces of white Elmer's Glue. (*That's* why it smells that way!)
- ❑ 1 1/4 cups of water
- ❑ 30 drops of food coloring (your choice)

1. Dissolve borax powder in 1/4 cup of warm water — set aside.
2. Stir together all the above, except the dissolving borax powder.
3. While rapidly stirring (naked fingers are de rigueur) add Borax mixture along the sides of the bowl. A slimy lump will begin to form. Continue to mix vigorously and the mixture will gel.
4. Remove the lump from the bowl and knead it for about 2 minutes. Done.

Keep KAG in an airtight container and if you love your family don't let it become one with clothing, hair or carpets. If KAG becomes stiff with use, dunk in water and moosh until it's original flexibilty is restored.

Hard to Believe, But True

In an earlier **Bag of Tricks** issue I had included some of these "educational" slips in syntax, concept and interpretation. To an educated person they are both flat-out funny, and sad. We can't do anything about the sad, so enjoy the funny.

The following is a selected anthology from a larger collection by Richard Lederer in *More Anguished English*.

❏ "One horsepower is the amount of energy it takes to drag a horse 500 feet in one second."

❏ "Our biology class went out to explore the swamp and collect little orgasms."

❏ "Pavlov studied the salvation of dogs."

❏ "My aunt won't be having any more kids because her tubes are tired."

❏ "A molecule is so small that it can't be seen by a naked observer."

❏ "Americans throw away tons of food that some Asian child could be eating."

❏ "Extinct birds lay very few eggs."

❏ "A porcupine is an animal with many pricks."

❏ "The pelvis protects the gentiles."

❏ "The heart beats faster when you are young, average when you are middle aged, hardly at all when you are old, and not at all when you are dead."

❏ "A circle is a round straight line with a hole in the middle."

❏ "To find the number of square feet in a room, you multiply the room by the number of feet."

❏ And finally, "The human body is composed of three parts: the Branium, the Borax, and the Abdominale Cavity. The Brainium contains the brain. The Borax contains the lungs, liver, and the living things. The Abdominale Cavity contains the bowels, of which there are five: A, E, I, O, and U."

...and that's the truth!

Jollys

Eric Johnson penned a few paragraphs about what he calls Jollys. I think you should hear about them, then seek out a few.

"A woman is cleaning a room in a hotel on the second floor. After consolidating the trash into a large plastic garbage bag, she steps out onto the balcony, peers down to the parking lot, checks the scene for observors and heaves that bag of garbage out into space to carve a graceful arc in the morning sunlight and land with a kerplop!, smack-dab in the middle of a humongous trash receptacle. She smiles unselfconsciously and walks back into the room to finish her work. What she did was get a Jolly, and a pretty good Jolly, I'd say!

A Jolly is that feeling of satisfaction you get when you do something just for fun. It's a small personal joy that borders briefly on glee. A Jolly will make you smile at the silliest things and would be a good measure of fun if the act itself weren't so subjective.

Jollys can be big or small. I think the cleaning lady got a small Jolly — perhaps bordering on big. Someone rolling a kayak in winter ocean water just for the fun of it, definitely gets a big Jolly.

I believe everyone needs to get a certain number of daily jollys, and apparently someone else agrees as evidenced by the saying, "...to get your Jollys."

The best part about getting your Jollys is that they are highly contagious. You can get a Jolly by seeing someone else get a Jolly. When I saw that maid smile, I realized that I had witnessed someone, "getting a little Jolly", and I got the same Jolly in the process. I'll bet you just got a vicarious Jolly just by reading about it."

I'm not sure what the moral implications are here, but it seems innocent enough. I'd assume that blatant Jollys are more acceptable than clandestine Jollys, but... that's not for me to say.

Ten Ways to Measure When You Don't Have a Ruler

1. Credit cards are usually 3 3/8" by 2 1/8"

2. Standard business cards are printed 3 1/2" by 2".

3. The standard 88 key piano board measures exactly 48 inches.

4. U.S. paper currency is 6 1/8" by 2 5/8".

5. The diameter of a quarter is approximately one inch, and the diameter of a penny is approximately 3/4".

6. A standard sheet of typing paper is 8 1/2" wide and 11" long.

7. A new wooden pencil is 7 1/2" long.

8. A Hershey's plain chocolate bar is ? long. This one's up to you.

10. The 3 by 5 card that you need to record all these off sized numbers on measures 3" X 5" — Surprise!

Tidbits

These **Tids** are **Bits** of essentially useless information that I've collected over time, but which are necessary to know in order to balance that plethora of frighteningly functional facts that weigh heavily and meaningfully on the psyche-side (left brain/right brain; your choice) of the cerebellum. I've listed the source of information when possible.

"People over 55 eat more ice cream per year than any other age group in the U.S., and the region with the highest per capita ice cream consumption is New England."

Speaking of ice cream, *Frusen Glädjè* means "frozen delight" in Swedish. *Häggen-Dazs* is a made-up promotional product name and has no meaning. I'll admit, that's minimally interesting, but actually I just wanted a reason to fool around with the computer Key Caps in the words Glädjé and Häggen.

á¡™£¢∞§¶•ªº≠œ∑®†¥¨^øπ‘''«ß∂ƒ©˙∆¬æ

— neat, huh?

Games Magazine and me

Oreos are the all-time best selling cookie, beating out other all-time favorites **Chips Ahoy!**, and **Fig Newtons**.

Gourmet Times

A capped jar of flies (say 15 of them) will weigh exactly the same whether the flies are sitting on the bottom of the jar or all flying at the same time.

Scientific American

Most people know that a *flock* of birds refers to a large number of congregated birds either in the air or on the ground, and that a large number of cattle are referred to as a *herd*. But did you know that a collection of apes is called a *shrewdness*? It's rare to see a *skulk* of foxes and even rarer to observe a *crash* of rhinos, but an *army* of frogs in springtime is expected. Would you need an assault rife to repel an *ambush* of tigers? From a distance it's hard to tell a *murder* of crows from an *unkindness* of ravens. Finally, you better keep your kitchen clean or you may have to put up with a *shit-load* of cockroaches.

Just kidding on that last one. You knew? Didn't fool you just a little? Come on!

It took Ashrita Furman 10.5 hours to forward somersault Paul Revere's midnight ride in reverse, (8,341 actual somersaults) to get into the *Guiness Book of World Records*. It took Paul Revere approximately one hour to make the ride from Charlestown to Lexington.

Yankee Magazine via Sue Shaefer

In a 1993 sanctioned distance ball event, Brian Pavlet drove a regulation golf ball 430 yards and 3 inches — a world's record. Longer distances have been recorded on ice, driving off a cliff, and on the moon, but...

United Airline's Hemisphere Magazine

"Ratio of the number of Americans who prefer toilet paper to unroll off the top to those who prefer the bottom: 3:1"

"An average 57% of magazines displayed in stores remain unsold."

"Cups of iceberg lettuce one must consume in order to satisfy the minimum daily requirement of *any* vitamin — twenty-seven and a half."

"Estimated number of standard sized helium balloons required to lift an American 10 year old off the ground — 2,450." Extrapolating that fact, it would take approximately 16,540 balloons to lift me off the ground.

"The heaviest kohlrabi ever grown weighed 62 lbs." It would take 1,820 balloons to lift this vegetable.

Harper's Index

There are 42 Florida Keys and they extend 150 miles into the Florida gulf from the tip of the mainland. There are 88 keys on a piano and they measure 48 inches from end to end.

Travel Brochure

"The poor coconut; 86% of a coconut's oil is saturated fat. Straight lard is only 38% saturated."

"A 3.5 oz. box of Goobers provides the consumer with 528 calories, and 34 grams of fat."

Nutrition Action Health Letter (5/94)

Gabriel Fallopius (1523-1562) fabricated the first condom out of linen.

Smithsonian Magazine

The "hand purse" (considered the national gesture of Italy and used in the game Italian Golf), actually signifies a question or fear.

Do's and Taboos Around The World
Roger Axtell

Did you know that you have been peeling bananas from the wrong end? Adam Clark (PA Intern, now working at The Hopkins School in New Haven, CT) pointed out that monkeys invariably start at the "other" end of the banana by pinching the tip, then peeling. After having struggled with the heavy stem end for over 50 years, I am pleased to tell you that Adam and the monkeys are right. You may never look at a banana in the same way again.

Another banana fillip. Use a blunt pointed object, (an oxymoron of profound proportions), like a knitting needle, to write your name or a short note (EAT ME!) on the side of an unpeeled banana. As you print the letters nothing will appear, but as the banana ripens (say overnight) the area that you bruised with the knitting needle will appear in dark letters. Leave messages for family members or someone at the super market.

"The erect penis of an adult gorilla measures about 1.25 inches in length. Compared with our ancestors' fixtures, the human penis is a veritable fire hose."

Esquire Magazine

"The lethal dose of caffeine in humans is estimated at about 10 grams, or the equivalent of 100 cups of coffee. One would have to drink 100 cups in one sitting, however, which doubtless accounts for the unpopularity of caffeine consumption as a means of taking one's own life."

Kenneth Davids

"Starbuck" was the coffee-loving first mate in Herman Melville's classic adventure tale, Moby Dick.

Starbucks Coffee Advert.

Footballs are not, and never were, made of pigskin.

Catgut strings do not come from cats. Sheep are usually the source.

There are only 46 states in the United States. VA, PA, KY, and MA are commonwealths.

Reader's Digest

Number of unused condoms discovered aboard a 53 man German submarine sunk during WW 11 — 2,000.

Funny Times

"In 1950 a group of climbers in Switzerland was followed to the top of the 14,691 foot Matterhorn by a four-month-old kitten."

Newspaper article

Notwithstanding what I said about *Tidbits* at the beginning of this erudite anthology, the following is useful information; might even keep you from getting a cat bite and/or scratch.

Research has recently determined that when cats roll onto their back and spread their legs, exposing their belly, they *do not* want you to scratch their vulnerable ventral. They are performing this as a submissive posture to other more dominating cats that says, "You are so big, and cool, and powerful, and I'm just a nothing under your feet. See, here's my bare tummy, do with me what you will — I cannot resist your greatness."

But, don't mistake this submissive belly-up pose as a cat's invitation to scratch and rub their underside. They are denigrating themselves to other, more dominating cats, hoping that by being such a wimp they don't get whacked about. If you take advantage of their embarrassing (that's probably anthropomorphic) belly-up position, they will chomp and strike your hand with impunity, 'cause you ain't no big honkin CAT.

Freely translated from DISCOVER magazine

Another interesting cat fact gleaned from a Scientific American magazine article on falling cats is that cats which fall or are tossed from high rise buildings are more likely to live if they fall from *above* ten stories. The reasoning is that once a cat orients its body into a falling position (much like the spread-eagle stablized sky diving position) and relaxes, the ground impact is much less damaging. Which, translated to a more practical situation, means that if you find yourself falling from over 100 feet, relax.

"Bull sperm frozen as long as 25 years has produced healthy, normal calves."

"A hard pencil can produce a line more than 30 miles long, whereas a jumbo refill ball point pen cartridge is rated at less than two miles."

A human takes approximately 500 million breaths in a lifetime. (I am committed to taking more than that, and big ones too! — KER)

70% of house dust consists of shed human skin.

OMNI Magazine

The dot over the letter i is called a *tittle*.

There are more sweat glands on the soles of your feet than any other part of your body. (That's why Tevas have a tendancy to develop a distinctive odor.)

In an average life time, the human body produces more than 25,000 quarts (6,250 gals.) of saliva. (Anybody have any stats on average life time urine output? That would certainly be of consuming interest.)

If the headwind is greater than a plane's maximum speed, the aircraft will fly backwards. (Unless it's headed straight down. — KER)

Anonymous; i.e., I forgot where I found these, so I didn't feel too badly about adding to them.

Nutsy

I was pretty sure that I had written about *Nutsy* at some point, but I checked with the machine here and it politely told me that "no matching items were found." I think it's lying, but I have no recourse except re-do Nutsy; which is OK because there's not much to say.

The following funn activity is based on something I did as a kid (...about six months ago — just kidding!) I wanted a bow and arrow but my parents didn't think it was a good idea (immaturity, lack of experience, shooting someone's eye out — type of thing). But I eventually got one because I was an only child, and then did exactly as I had been asked not to do (there were lots of things that I was told not to do, this just happened to be one of them).

Someone (probably a parent) told me not to shoot arrows straight up. They probably even told me why, but it seemed like a great thing to do. After launching the arrow and watching it go up, up, up; getting smaller and smaller and smaller, I knew why I was asked not to do this. RUN AWAY! RUN AWAY!!!

In an attempt to reproduce this exciting nostalgic scenario, let me

introduce you to *Nutsy*. After having played with Comet or Rasta Balls, (check out Rasta Balls in the index or Comet Balls in **Bottomless Bag Again !?**; pg. 68) ask your group to bring their spinning ball and stand in a comfortable cluster in an open field. A comfortable cluster is defined as close enough to enjoy the action, but not so close that you will get whacked with a spinning ball.

Standing and individually spinning, the group releases their balls straight up on the count of three; you know, like one, two, THREE! After the release DO NOT LOOK UP, look wide-eyed at someone else. Just so you have something to do with your hands, since the ball is gone, put them on top of your head. Remain in this position until gravity has once again fulfilled its potential and you have experienced the full "raining balls" effect of Nutsy. You can do this again.

No score, no rules, just funn.

Whoops Johnny...

Another bit of verbal/digital manipulation that fits in with other demonstrations of this vertical/lateral thinking genre, *(Hands Down, I've Got the Beat, Passing Crossed or Uncrossed*, etc.)

The idea here is to present something visual to the audience that is easy to duplicate, then indicate that if an individual would like to join your *verrry* exclusive club all they have to do is replicate exactly what you just demonstrated.

You need to know that whatever you visually and verbally demonstrate is just a distraction. The real key to *joining the club* is something that you do either prior to starting the visual demo, or immediately after.

Do this — Hold up one of your hands so that your palm is about 18" from your face. Separate your fingers. Using the index finger of your other hand touch that finger to the pinky of the hand in front of your face, at the same time saying "Johnny". Touch the next finger (ring finger) with the same index finger, and say "Johnny" again. Continue this Johnny-Johnny sequence until the two index fingers touch, then slide the index finger of the right hand down the side of the left index finger, continuing up the slope of the thumb to the tip of the thumb. From the beginning this would sound like: "Johnny, Johnny, Johnny, Johnny, Whoops Johnny", (your right index finger is now on top of the left thumb). Reverse direction with another "Whoops Johnny" and continue Johnnying back to the little finger where you started.

Before you start the first "Johnny", subtly clear your throat, which is, of course, the key to joining the club; all the Johnny, Johnny... stuff is pure window dressing.

As much fun as this can become (particularly for you, 'cause you know the answer), don't present more than two of these "what's the key" activities at one session. Not being able to figure out what's going on twice in a row may add to an insecure person's already negative attitude about their personal capabilities. Also, don't forget to tell everyone what the answer to the puzzle is before going on to something else.

Even if you think that everyone knows the gimmick, verbalize the answer because invariably there will be a couple folks still dumbfounded but not willing to admit it.

If you need some rationale as to how come your playing "mind" games, try this:

❑ By this time in the program you have probably presented more than one initiative problem. Groups and the individuals in those groups have a tendancy to approach problem solving with blinders on, holding on to what seems to be a possible answer and not letting go. They, or someone, impulsively gets hold of an idea and follows it blindly right or wrong. "Johnny, Johnny...", indicates that thinking beyond the obvious solution is the most efficient way to approach an initiative situation; vertical vs lateral thinking. If the group remembers the lesson learned as the result of "failing forward" in this situation, the next problem solving circumstance might be better handled.

❑ In almost every social situation there seems to be an "in" group that's *in the know*, and a larger group that wishes they knew what was going on or would like to be part of that shared social structure. When a person finally comes up with the answer to these "what's the key" puzzlers, they become part of that intimate elite, sharing the laughs and knowing smiles. The people who are stumped and not part of the club become more and more frustrated and even angry about being excluded. The feelings generated by these exercises are real, poignant, and transferable. Take the time to share comments from both sides of "the club".

The Centurions

As of this writing I'm 58, and Adrian Kissler is 56. We make up *The Centurions;* i.e., two slightly older guys whose combined ages easily top the century mark.

Adrian and I have known each other since we were in the Army together at Ft. Sam Houston, Texas; c. 1960. Since that time we have on occasion hiked, camped, worked, played, competed, and built ropes courses together.

Our most recent ropes course extravaganza took place at Alpine Christian Conference Center in Blue Jay, California. Blue Jay, at 6,000+ feet elevation, is just down the road from Big Bear, both located in the San Bernardino Mountains of Southern California.

Ade and I had done some work there last year installing a super-fast zip line, so we were ready to escalate the challenge, and Camp Alpine sure had the trees; Douglas Firs that easily topped 150' were in abundance. Eddie Passmore, the ropes course coordinator at the center had expressed a desire for "something different" on the course, maybe "something really high".

As a former full time ropes course builder, mostly on the East coast, I had always wanted to build a Pamper Pole or Plank over 100 feet high, but the trees of the Eastern biome just didn't allow for that type of escalated planning. Well, maybe a few did, but I'm talking about useable trunk diameter, not just the tree's tippy top.

The trees in Blue Jay were not only high enough, but grew in close enough proximity to one another that it wasn't difficult to scope out three humongous trees arranged in a triangular pattern that allowed engineering a climb to an extended platform (plank) and dive to an "inconveniently" hung trapeze.

The following photo shows what we accomplished, "something different and really high". Eddie decided that an appropriate name for the climb and dive was **The Centurion**. *The Centurions* could not have agreed more.

Stats

Trees — All three; Douglas Fir

Platform height — 100' and change

Platform length from the tree — 8' 3"

Belay cable height — 111'

Belay rope (12mm KM 3) — 235'

Belay device — A stripped cedar Jus-rite Descender

Trapeze jump distance — Approx. 7′ out and 5′ up.

1/2″ staples used — 166

Current climbing record to the platform — 59+ seconds

"Quarterly" Quotes

Why a section on quotes? Simply for your enjoyment or ignorement. For over sixteen years *Quarterly Quotes* was a regular subscription feature of **Bag of Tricks**. The following quotes are not arranged in any particular way, nor collected with any goal in mind except that they pleased me at the moment I read or heard them. I hope they also make you smile or pause to contemplate the joys, satirical twists and existential contradictions in our lives.

"The greatest accomplishments in science and the arts have been made by individuals acting alone. No park has a statue dedicated to a committee."

"No failure is ever final."

"Middle age is when you have two choices and you choose the one that gets you home earlier."

"A person in love sometimes mistakes a pimple for a dimple."

"If you see a turtle on top of a fence post, remember he had some help getting there." (*I really like this quote. Anyone know who said it?*)

"You have two choices for dinner. Take it or leave it."

"It's hard to argue with someone when they are right."

"Avoid $1,000 meetings to solve $100 problems."

"Enthusiasm is caught, not taught."

"Motel mattresses are better on the side away from the phone."

"If you give a pig and a boy everything they want, you'll get a good pig and a bad boy."

"Women with double first names usually make terrific peach cobbler."

Anonymous

"Happiness is nothing more than health and a poor memory."

Albert Schweitzer

"The reverse side also has a reverse side."

Japanese Saying

"The more creative you become the more insignificant things you notice."

KER

"Age doesn't matter, unless you are cheese."

Billie Burke

"How old would you be, if you didn't know how old you was?"

Sachel Paige

"To be an effective adventure game leader you gotta recognize the value of shared stupidity."

Jim Moll

"We do not believe in ourselves until someone reveals that deep inside us something is valuable, worth listening to, worthy of our trust, sacred to our touch. Once we believe in ourselves we can risk curiosity, wonder, spontaneous delight or any experience that reveals the human spirit."

e.e. cummings

"Humor (Adventure) can be dissected, as a frog can, but the thing dies the process."

E.B. White

"It's just not F N without U."

Greeting Card

"Beware Brutus, lest we cleave to one another as mawkish players, so intent on our own desires that we scatter the pureness of our intent."

Clavidicus

Sylvia's Lament

"My friends have not seen London,
They've never been to France,
But yesterday at recess
They saw my underpants

I've thought a lot about it.
This conclusion I have drawn:
I'm embarrassed that they saw them,
But I'm glad I had them on."

Bill Dodds

"Remember you are all alone in the kitchen and no one can see you."

Julia Child

"When you are in love with someone, you want to be near him all the time, except when you are out buying things and charging them to him"

Miss Piggy

"Anyone seen on a bus after the age of thirty has been a failure in life."

The Dutchess of Westminster

"Cats are smarter than dogs. You can't get eight cats to pull a sled through snow."

Jeff Valdez

"Cats are intended to teach us that not everything in nature has a function."

Garrison Keillor

"I should warn you that underneath these clothes I'm wearing boxer shorts and I know how to use them."

Robert Orben

"A venturesome minority will always be eager to get off on their own... let them take risks, for Godsake, let them get lost, sunburnt, stranded, drowned, eaten by bears, buried alive under avalanches—that is the right and privilege of any free American."

Idaho Law Review 407, 1980

"Nature is filled with gravity."

Mountain Biking — "...a mode of transportation that combines the strenuousness of continuous pushups with the comfort of falling down a flight of steps in a shopping cart."

Newsweek 7/19/93

"As a postscript, take time to laugh at yourself, with others, and even at the occasional absurdity of life itself. Use your imagination to discover the weird, invent the bizarre, and fully appreciate the mundane in all matters. Play with life at times as if it were all part of a personal Candid Camera scenario, which requires that, in the end, you smile because living well is the best revenge."

Psychology & Life college text - by Zimbardo

"An enormous problem is that people do not build enough relaxation, alternative creativity, or pleasure into their work lives. Our collective nose is too close to the grindstone."

Malcolm Boyd

There is a certain type of person who refuses to grow old, who tenaciously but also naturally clings to childhood all their life. They are relentlessly inquisitive, buffoonish, cocksure, compulsively spontaneous, optimistic, gullible, impetuous, reckless, exuberant, moody, occasionally ill tempered, charming, often corny, and who possesses an uncanny sense of play. They are the children who never got tamed, those who resisted **adult**eration, considering that "an adult is simply a broken down child."

A paraphrase from Roger Rosenblatt and quote from Piers Anthony

"People learn best when entertained greatly while being educated gently."

Commodore Longfellow

"It's important to have an end to journey towards, but it's the journey that matters in the end."

Ursula Le Guinn

"The memories of my family outings are still a source of strength to me. I remember we'd pile into the car —I forget what kind it was — and drive and drive. I'm not sure where we'd go, but I think there were some trees there. The smell of something was strong in the air as we played whatever sport we played. I remember a bigger, older guy we called "Dad". We'd eat some stuff, or not, and then I think we went home.

I guess some things never leave you."

Jack Handey

"Rank of cola, breakfast cereal, and ground beef, among the groceries Americans spend most on each year: 1, 2, & 3."

"Ratio of the number of Americans who prefer toilet paper to unroll off the top to those who prefer the bottom: 3:1"

Harper's Index

"Americans do not live well with failure; we have made a national fetish of success and victory."

"Few people learn from success, but there is often much to learn from failure."

Steven Muller

"Winter is not a season, it's an occupation."

Sinclair Lewis

Difference between the ideal and the real — as pertains to adults participating in play."

ideal - spontaneous
real - planned, expensive, self-serving, win/lose competition

KER

"The Golden Mean: This is an intermediate point lying somewhere between, "if at first you don't succeed, try, try again", and "enough is enough".

"Being in love is better than being in jail, a dentist's chair, or a holding pattern over Philadelphia — but not if he doesn't love you back."

"Strength: Strength is the capacity to break a Hershey bar into four pieces with your bare hands — and then eat just one of the pieces."

Judith Viorst

"Don't accept your dog's admiration as conclusive evidence that you are wonderful."

Ann Landers

"You throw away the outside and cook the inside. Then you eat the outside and throw away the inside. What is it? (corn on the cob)

Anonymous

"Your childhood isn't lost, you just misplaced it."

KEDS Commercial

About Antarctic travel by foot: "The cleanest and most isolated way of having a bad time ever devised..."

Robert Swan

"Treating the symptoms of a disease is like killing the messenger for bringing bad news."

Stephen Cummings

"We can only regret that the twentieth century, with its passive attitude towards the spending of leisure time, has replaced most recreational activities, both for young and old, with one, singular, international occupation — television. Even the parlour game has been swallowed up and regurgitated as a commercial operation. Even parties are beamed into homes as a substitute for the real thing, to be passively watched rather than actively engaged in by a generation of children who are in danger of forgetting how to play."

Patrick Beaver — Victorian
Parlour Games For Today

"Basically my wife was immature. I'd be at home in the bath and she'd come and sink my boats."

"I can't understand why more people aren't bisexual. It would double your chances for a date on Saturday night."

Woody Allen

"My wife doesn't care what I do when I'm away, as long as I don't have a good time."

Lee Trevino

"A man must be potent and orgasmic to ensure the future of the race. A woman need only be available."

Masters and Johnson

"Men play the game, women know the score."

Roger Woods

"All men laugh at the Three Stooges and all women think that the Three Stooges are assholes."

Jay Leno

"I only like two kinds of men: domestic and imported."

Mae West

"We sleep in separate rooms, we have dinner apart, we take separate vacations—we're doing everything we can to keep our marriage together."

Rodney Dangerfield

"We would have broken up except for the children. Who are the children? Well, she and I were."

Mort Sahl

"If you believe you can, you're right. If you believe you can't, you're right again."

Anonymous

"If you process too much you're going to end up with Velveeta cheese."

passed along by Rhonda Aubry